JESUS: THE MAN AND THE MESSAGE

I dedicate this book with thanks and with love,
to the organisers and helpers of the
Handicapped Children's Group, Christ the King parish,
Bromborough, Wirral (Liverpool).
Being with them in Lourdes recently,
and witnessing their extraordinary love 'for the least of these',
has helped me enormously in making the gospel message
real and tangible, in a credible and very evident way.
My special thanks to my sister, Ann Cooper,
who was instrumental in putting me in touch
with such a 'pearl of great price'.

Jack McArdle SS CC

Jesus:
The Man and the Message

the columba press

First published in 1997 by
the columba press
55a Spruce Avenue, Stillorgan Industrial Park,
Blackrock, Co Dublin

Cover by Bill Bolger
Origination by The Columba Press
Printed in Ireland by
Colour Books Ltd, Dublin
ISBN 185607 207 X

Contents

Introduction

For many years now, I have been endeavouring in my own tin-pot way to devolve some sort of new theological language for expressing concepts and truths that, in themselves, can be abstruse and abstract. In this book the process continues, but with one major difference. This book is about Jesus, who is anything but abstract, and whose message is anything but abstruse. Incarnation has given us a God with flesh and blood just as we are; someone who walked our world, and who sailed our waters (not to mention walking on the waters as well!). He came as a child, he spoke to children and about children, and he invited us to get in touch with the Inner Child within all of us, if we hoped to discover a proper response to his message. Such a discovery would be the beginning of the process of total recovery into life in abundance.

These reflections are quite personal, which is a quality I try to preserve in whatever I write. I can say, without any desire to be pretentious, that the person of Jesus fascinates me. I experience a constant futility in trying to grasp the scope of his simplicity, and the wholeness that his life exemplifies. I see him as extremely courageous, with very clear convictions about truth, and how it should be taught and lived. He spoke with great fervour, something that goes with knowing what one is talking about. I don't wish to border on the factitious here, like the person who began his talk with the words, 'As Jesus said, and rightly so ...'! I do, however, allow myself the freedom to express something of what I admire in him, in his personality, and in his message. When I look at the ocean, I can see a vast expanse of water. I must remember, however, that all I can see is the surface of the water, and not the millions and millions of gallons that lie beneath that surface. Like St John, I can write only 'what I see', and humbly accept the fact that my vision is as limited as the horizon determined by God's Spirit. I have enjoyed writing reflections on Jesus as a teacher, as a friend, as a rebel. In the very best sense of the word, he could really stir things up! I could never imagine myself being bored in his presence, because of the inner bubbling enthusiasm he exuded. When he spoke of the Spirit being a fountain of living water rising up from within, he exemplified that in a clear and credible way. He spoke the word that challenged, as well as the word of comfort and compassion. He was prepared to comfort the afflicted, and to afflict the comfortable. In himself, he is a person who leads, and his message is one to follow. He was totally unambiguous and uncomplicated in his living and in his teaching.

Knowing about Jesus must lead us to know him in a personal way. He himself is his greatest message. In the history of salvation, he is God's final and definitive message and invitation. That invitation always evokes a response, even if it is one of indifference. We have to decide one way or another. 'You are either for me, or against me', he said. He came for the fall, as well as for the resurrection of many. There is not one might or maybe throughout the whole gospel. He came to do and to teach, and in that order. He is the greatest role model ever given us in the living out of our own lives. He is not manipulating or demanding. All he asks for is goodwill, and for this he promises peace on earth. In presenting these reflections, I depend totally on his Spirit to make use of the words I use, and the views I express. May you, the reader, be truly blessed in the reading.

1 The Message

Throughout the Old Testament, God spoke to his people in many ways. He spoke through the prophets, and he spoke through nature. The words spoken through the prophets were sometimes words of condemnation, at other times words of encouragement and promise. He spoke in the wind, he spoke in the rain, and, as the Psalmist puts it, the mountains, the seas, and the skies proclaimed his presence and his glory. The Hebrews had a sense of God being very near to them. The Old Testament is chock-full of accounts of how God intervened in their lives, either to rescue or to punish. Essentially, they were a pagan people who, even after accepting the Ten Commandments, were still reluctant to let go of their pagan gods. They complained a lot, and were continually putting God to the test. They were a 'head-strong people', to use God's own words. They were 'stubborn and stiff-necked', which was another of God's opinions about them. God was continually calling them to turn back to him with all their hearts. Through promise, invitation, reprimand, and threat, God endeavoured to keep them in line. He had given them free will, so he would not attempt to compel them, or to coerce them into anything against their will.

The message of God was, essentially, an invitation to return to the garden. It is important to understand how our relationship with God is set up. God loves us. That is the core and the nub of the message. An essential ingredient in creation is love. Love, by definition, is always creative. In an ideal world, all babies would be conceived and procreated in love. God is love. In other words, God cannot do anything but love us, and 100% at that. If a problem comes into the relationship, it always comes from us. Each one of us is the loose cannon in this relationship.

I could predict that, at a certain moment, on a certain day, during a certain year, the sun, moon, and earth would be in a straight line, forming an eclipse. I could not predict how a particular person might act or react, with anything like the same accuracy! Only God is constant, only God is consistent. It is part of our nature to be always in a constant state of change. Alice in Wonderland begins her story with the words, 'I could tell you my story beginning this morning. I could not begin yesterday, because I was a different person then.' When I was learning my catechism many years ago, I was told that 'God is immutable'. I hadn't a clue just what that meant! I now know that it means 'God does not change'. God is the same yesterday, today, and always. God is Creator. He will never destroy this world of ours. We're on the way to doing that ourselves!

God's original offer is still there, even if we have walked away from it, or turned our backs on it. The garden is still there for us. In other words, we are invited to return to the garden, and to walk humbly with our God. The prophet Micah told the people, 'The Lord has already told you what is good, and this is what he requires of you: to do what is right, to love mercy, and to walk humbly with your God.'

God is love, and a central ingredient of love is forgiveness. Just as God's love is infinite and unconditional, so is his forgiveness. Time and time again, through the prophets, God called his people to return to him. 'Though your sins are like scarlet, I will make them white as snow.' Through the prophet Hosea, God made the following appeal to his people, which I quote at some length, because of the beautiful insight it reveals:

Return to your God, O Israel. Your sins have caused your downfall. Return to God with humble words. Say to him, 'Oh you who show compassion to the fatherless, forgive our sin, be appeased'… I will heal their wavering, and love them with all my heart, for my anger has turned from them.

I believe it is well worth while listening to the words of some of the prophets, in order to appreciate God's deep longing for his people to return to his love and friendship. In doing so, we notice once again the basic stubbornness of the human heart. The prophets were accepted as being the voice of God, and yet their message was so often ignored and went unheeded. The words of the prophets are with us to this day, so they were not just the verbal meanderings of some individuals. Because I am a teacher, I never presume that another understands every word I say! Therefore, I wish to preface my quotations from the prophets with the following clarifications: Because the Hebrews considered God's name to be holy, they always referred to God as Yahweh, which literally means 'I am who am'. When God spoke to them he called them Israel, Judah, people of Zion (a holy mountain), or he spoke to their leader on their behalf. Isaiah spoke the following words on behalf of Yahweh, the all-holy God:

> Yahweh waits to give you grace; he rises to show you compassion. For Yahweh is a God of justice. Blessed are all who wait for him. O People of Zion, who dwell in Jerusalem, you will weep no more. When you cry, he will listen; when he hears, he will answer … the Lord will hide no longer. Your own eyes will see him, and your ear will listen to his words, whispering: This is the way, walk in it.

Perhaps the most hope-filled message from Yahweh, and one that clearly predicts the coming of a future Messiah, is found in Isaiah 35:

> The wilderness and the arid land will rejoice, the desert will be glad and blossom. … Give vigour to weary hands, and strength to weary knees. Say to those who are afraid: Have courage, do not fear. See, your God comes, demanding justice. He is the God who rewards, the God who

comes to save you. Then will the eyes of the blind be opened, and the ears of the deaf unsealed. Then will the lame leap as a hart, and the tongue of the dumb sing and shout. For water will break out in the wilderness, and streams will gush forth from the desert. The thirsty ground will become a pool, and arid lands springs of water. In the haunts where once reptiles lay, grass will grow with reeds and rushes. There will be a highway, which will be called The Holy Highway. No one unclean will pass over it, nor any wicked fool stray there. No lion will be found there, nor any beast of prey. Only the redeemed will walk there. For the ransomed of Yahweh will return, with everlasting joy crowning their heads. They will come to Zion singing, gladness and joy marching with them, while sorrow and sighing flee away.

I would like to stick with Isaiah for another while, because it contains so many messages of future hope:

You are my servant, I have chosen you, not cast you away. Fear not, for I am with you; be not dismayed, for I am your God. I will give you strength, I will bring you help, I will uphold you with the right hand of my justice. ... For I, Yahweh, your God, take hold of your right hand, and say to you: Fear not, I will help you. ... The poor and the afflicted seek water, and find none. Their tongues are parched, with nothing to drink. But I, Yahweh, will hear them; I, the God of Israel, will not forsake them. I will open up streams over the barren heights, and let the rivers flow through all the valleys; I will turn the desert into lakes and brooks, and a thirsty earth into a land of springs ... that all may see and know, consider and understand, that the hand of Yahweh has done this, that the Holy One of Israel has created this.

I must now resist the temptation to quote more and more such powerful messages of hope, spoken through the prophet Isaiah. The Old Testament is like coming events throwing their shadow. The Old Testament is like radio, while the New Testament is like television. The promises of the Old are fulfilled in the New, and the words of love are accompanied by hugs and tears.

Jeremiah spoke these words on behalf of Yahweh:

If you return, I will take you back, and you will serve me again. Draw the gold from the dross, and you will be as my own mouth. I am with you to free you and save you. I will redeem you from the wicked, and free you from the hands of tyrants. ... Alas for the shepherds who mislead and scatter the sheep of my pasture. You have scattered my sheep, and driven them away, instead of caring for them. Now I will deal with you because of your evil deeds. I will gather the rest of my sheep from every land to which I have driven them, and I will bring them back to the grasslands. They will be fruitful, and increase in number. I will place shepherds over them who will care for them. No longer will they fear or be terrified. No one will be lost. The day is coming when I will raise up to David a righteous offspring, a king who will rule wisely, and govern with justice and righteousness. Then Judah will enjoy peace, and Israel will live in safety.

The following passage from Jeremiah is worth quoting for its poetry as much as for its loving invitation to the people to come back to God:

Hear the word of Yahweh, O nations, proclaim it on distant coastlands: He who scattered Israel now gathers them together; he guards them as a shepherd guards his flock. For Yahweh shall ransom Jacob, and redeem him from the hands of his conqueror. Shouting for joy, they will ascend Zion; they will come streaming to Yahweh's blessings – the grain, the new wine and the oil, the young of the flocks and the herds. They will be like a well-watered garden; no more will they be afflicted. Maidens will make merry and dance, young men and old as well. I will turn their mourn-

ing into gladness. Instead of sorrow I will give them comfort and joy.'

And now we turn to the prophet Ezekiel to hear some more
of the Lord's promises:

As the shepherd looks after his flock when he finds them
scattered, so will I watch over my sheep, and gather them
from all the places where they were scattered in a time of
cloud and fog. I will bring them out from the nations, and
gather them from other countries ... I will search for the
lost, and bring back the strays. I will bind up the injured,
and strengthen the weak ... They will know that I,
Yahweh, am their God, and that I am with them.

Perhaps the most reassuring promise of all is contained in the
following words:

I will gather you from all the nations, and bring you back
to your own land. I shall pour pure water over you, and
you shall be made clean. I will give you a new heart, and
put a new spirit within you. I shall remove your heart of
stone and give you a heart of flesh. I will put my spirit
within you, and move you to follow my decrees and keep
my laws. You will live in the land I gave your forefathers;
you shall be my people, and I shall be your God.

Ezekiel was given a direct commission in the following
words:

My people say 'It is the end of us, our hope is gone'.
Prophesy! Say to them: 'This is what Yahweh says: "I am
going to open your graves, I shall bring you out of your
graves, my people, and lead you back to the land of Israel.
You will know that I am Yahweh, O my people, when I
open your graves, and bring you out of your graves, when
I put my spirit in you, and you live. I shall settle you in
your land, and you will know that I, Yahweh, have done
what I said I would do."'

Before drawing this chapter to a close and to a conclusion, I would like to quote a few words from the prophet Hosea. Through this prophet, God said that Israel had prostituted herself, and no longer could be called his spouse. However, in his great love, he desires to lure her back to him and to his love:

> I am going to allure her, lead her once more into the desert, where I can speak to her tenderly. Then I will give back her vineyards ... Yahweh says: she will call me my husband ... You will be my spouse forever, betrothed in justice and integrity; we will be united in love and tenderness. I will espouse you in faithfulness, and you will come to know Yahweh.

The final words of Hosea form a strong plea to return to God, Yahweh:

> Return to your God Yahweh, O Israel! Your sins have caused your downfall. Return to Yahweh with humble words. Say to him: 'Oh you who show compassion to the fatherless, forgive our sin, be appeased. Instead of bulls and sacrifices, accept the praise from our lips.' I will heal their wavering, and love them with all my heart, for my anger has turned from them. I shall be like dew to Israel, like the lily will he blossom.

Thank you, dear reader, for bearing with me thus far! I felt it necessary to paint some kind of backdrop to the main theme of this book. Throughout history, God continued to call his people to return to him. His final messenger was Jesus himself. Jesus would accuse them for ignoring the prophets, and for killing many of them. He would tell a story about a king who sent messengers, one after another, and each was rejected. The king then decided, 'I will send my son. Surely they will heed him.'

2 The Messenger

God is love. God cannot not love me. Even if I ended up in hell, God's love has not changed. It is just that I have chosen to put myself outside his love. There is a light overhead here as I write. I can go out the door, however, and walk into the darkness. Nothing in this room will have changed, and the light will still be shining. God gives me nothing; he offers me everything. I am totally free to accept or reject. That is the nature of love; it must never impinge on the freedom and the free will of the other.

God will not send me anywhere when I die. Rather will he eternalise the direction my life is now taking. From the first moment of human rebellion, it has always been God's desire to invite us back to the garden. We saw that in the words of the prophets in chapter one.

Now, finally, God sent his greatest and most personal invitation, Jesus. If we reject Jesus, we reject God who sent him. Jesus is both the messenger and the message. He is Emmanuel, God-among-us. 'They who see me, see the Father; they who hear me, hear the Father. The Father and I are one.' In other words, if you reject me, you reject the one who sent me; and if you reject my message, you are rejecting the messenger who brings you that message.

If Jesus were on this earth for three minutes, instead of thirty-three years, I believe he would have told us the story of the Prodigal Son, or what could well be called the Forgiving Father. In simple language, Jesus is saying 'Come home, even if you got pig's food all over your face. There is a big welcome and a hug waiting for you.' That is a summary of the gospel message. 'Come back to me with all your heart. Don't let fear keep us apart. Long have I waited for your coming home to me, and living deep within my love.'

Jesus is the Father's messenger, and he is the Father's message. The invitation is to nothing less than full entry into the family of God. Jesus tells many a parable about people being invited to a meal. For anyone who wants to listen and hear, the message is very very simple. 'They who have ears to hear, let them hear.' Once again Jesus, the teacher, brings them from something with which they were all familiar, to another truth, at a much deeper level. An invitation, by definition, implies courtesy, and nothing that smacks of coercion or manipulation. An invitation always demands and always receives a response. We may put RSVP all over it, but, even when no reply arrives, that silence, in itself, is a reply. That is the wonderful thing about an invitation. It just won't go away, and, should I choose to ignore it, I cannot deny or cover-up that fact. In an ideal world, the invitation, once issued, frees the sender from any other obligation. If my intended guests are not free to stay away, then I wonder how free they will be if they arrive. Naturally, of course, we are all human, and part of ourselves may go with the invitation. If the invitation is rejected or ignored, we ourselves feel rejected and ignored. That is why I prefaced earlier comments with the words 'In an ideal world'.

God sends an invitation, and he comes in person to deliver it. How he did this, and how that invitation was accepted and rejected is what the gospels are about. 'He came to his own and his own received him not. For to those who did receive him, he gave the right to become children of God. All they had to do was trust him to save them.'

Once again, I repeat that the invitation is to become nothing less than children of God. We are all familiar with the process of adoption. There are many factors at play here, not least being the permission of the natural mother and/or father. The only central figure not involved in any of the decision-making is the baby. Regarding the invitation from God, however, the only ones involved are God and myself. To summarise the words of Jesus, 'My Father will be your Father, if you become as little children'. I will examine this in greater detail later in this chapter.

There are two sides to every agreement. In Jesus, the Father has put down a very clear and distinct marker about where he stands. His invitation is clear and unambiguous, and his commitments and promises are unconditional. I honestly believe that the quality of my own response is inspired and deeply effected by my growing awareness of the Father's side of the agreement or covenant. 'In this is love', says John, 'not that we love God but he has first loved us.' In other words, the saints are not those who love God, but those who are totally convinced that God loves them. It is vital for us to constantly remember that the whole idea was God's in the first place.

Being the inheritors of the fall-out from original sin, it would be no problem at all for us to take over the whole show, and turn the divine initiative into human endeavour. I cannot respond until I have received and considered the invitation. Repentance, conversion, surrender – and all that is part of what we bring to God – is our response to the invitation. 'Come back to me with all your hearts.' 'Come to me all you who are burdened and heavily laden....'

In the Old Testament, God, through Moses, issued the following invitation, or offered the following covenant (agreement): 'I will be your God if you will be my people.' This was offered to a pagan people, who were capable of producing a god of their own at a mere whim. Like any offer or invitation, it put the other in a position which called for a response. In the New Testament, God, through Jesus, offered a new covenant and issued a whole new invitation: 'I will be your Father if you become my children.' Jesus emphasised this by telling us that, unless we become as little children, we cannot enter his kingdom. It was to establish that kingdom that Jesus

came. Herod asked him, 'Are you a king?' and Jesus replied,
'Yes, I am, and that is why I came. But my kingdom is not of
this world.'

One of the many things that have changed over the years is
how children celebrate a birthday. Presence at the party today
is by invitation only! For the child concerned, the excitement
begins with the issuing of the invitations. It is certainly not an
open invitation. There is a definite selective process in oper-
ation. On the other hand, we all are familiar with functions to
which there is an open invitation. There is no hierarchy or
order of merit. Anyone who receives or reads the invitation is
free to come along on the day. In our way of thinking, this is
seen as something of lesser importance. It is, literally, a free-
for-all, and the idea of invitation is seen as nothing more than
an advertisment. When there is an open invitation, there
surely will be something on sale and, perhaps, a few raffle
tickets!

The invitation of the gospel is unique. In a way it is a free-
for-all, while being singularly personal and individual. 'Who
do people say that I am? ... Who do you say that I am?' is one
of the more central questions of Jesus. Jesus is a very personal
God. I must never presume that he is somewhere in the
community, in the crowd. Mary and Joseph did that, only to
arrive home and discover that he wasn't there at all!
Christianity is, essentially, about a personal encounter with
Jesus Christ, an acceptance of his message, and a willingness
to live it. On more than one occasion Jesus confronts us with a
direct personal question, 'Will you also go away?' 'Do you
love me more than these?' Entering into this personal relationship is the journey of the Christian.

The shepherds were told the message by an angel, and yet
they said, 'Let us go to Bethlehem and see this thing which the
Lord has made known to us.' The woman at the well brought
out her friends to meet Jesus, and they ended up telling her,
'Now we believe, not because you told us, but because we
have seen for ourselves.' The early followers of Jesus asked

him, 'Where do you live?' and he replied 'Come and see for yourselves.' That invitation still stands.

How many people believe the truths of the gospel because they learned them in school? That's hardly good enough! If I were to die this moment, it would make sense to me if Jesus looked me straight in the eye and asked, 'Did you yourself really come to know that my Father loved you, or did you believe it on the word of another?' After curing several people, Jesus asked that they not publicise that fact. On first reading, that seems strange. On reflection, I like to think that Jesus is saying, 'Don't tell anyone, because I don't want them believing in me because you were cured. I want them to come and experience my healing for themselves and in themselves.'

'Word' can mean many things. It can be a word, as in a dictionary, and be something made up of letters to help give expression to something. We can ask, 'Have you received any word from John yet?' and in this case it means a message, a letter, a communication of some kind. It can mean an announcement when we say that the final word has been spoken, and a promise, when another gives us an undertaking 'on his word'.

Jesus is the Word of God. He is all of the above definitions. He is God's message, his announcement, his promise. God is love, and Jesus is love incarnate, is love made up of a human body, with all the attributes of our human nature. Because of the involvement of human nature, Jesus is a Word spoken in our language. He does not need an interpreter, because the message comes complete with the gift of wisdom, discernment, knowledge, and understanding. The paradox is that, in our head-world, in our world of human understanding, the message makes absolutely no sense, is absolute nonsense! It is part of the mystery of God not to be capable of subjection to the laboratories of our minds. 'I thank you, Father, for concealing this from the intellectual and worldly-wise, and revealing it to mere children,' was the prayer of Jesus.

There is a legend, that would not want to be taken too lit-

erally. It speaks of God enjoying the company of Adam and
Eve in the garden. He spoke words of love and of belonging
to them. They were the focal point of his attention and interest.
At an unguarded moment, the devil appeared and gagged
God's tongue, which prevented him from speaking. Many
centuries later, God indicated to Satan that he wished to
speak only one word. Satan considered this for a while. He
felt that one word couldn't do much harm to the grip he had
established on things and, so, he agreed. God's tongue was
untied, and he whispered just one word, 'Jesus'. Right there
all the work of Satan, all his bondages on people, all his control of God's creation, came crashing to the ground. His reign
was over, the tables were turned, and God's original creation
was restored. Jesus is the *Word* of God. Jesus is the final, complete, and eternal word of God.

I find St John, apostle and evangelist, a very interesting
study. He was with Jesus from the beginning. He was certain
of Jesus' love, calling himself 'the beloved disciple', 'the disciple Jesus loved'. His chapters on the final discourse of Jesus
at the Last Supper capture the beauty and the simplicity of it
all. Many years later, as an old man on the island of Patmos,
he wrote his letters, which are sheer poetry. He had reduced
the whole gospel to one simple phrase, 'Little children, let us
love one another, because God loves us. If we live in love, we
live in God, and God lives in us.' His gospel account is probably the most studied and discussed of all four gospels. He begins with a crescendo, with an outpouring of proclamation,
that can leave one gasping.

Some years ago an American space shuttle was travelling
around the moon. There were many anxious moments for all
concerned as the shuttle was on the other side of the moon,
and, therefore, unable to make contact with base. The great
moment that attracted the attention of the world was when
the shuttle caught sight of earth again, and one of the astro-
nauts read the opening words of John's gospel: 'In the beginning was the Word, and the Word was with God, and the

Word was God.' It is not unreasonable to say that John probably knew and understood Jesus better than any of the other
apostles. He was with Jesus from the beginning. He was one
of the chosen few who went with Jesus when he went aside
from time to time. He was with Jesus on Thabor and in
Gethsemane. His grasp of the truth about eucharist was complete. He gives the miracle of the loaves, the long discourse
on the bread of life, and the details of the Last Supper. He felt
so close to Jesus and so at ease with him, that he considered
himself to be a special friend. When he comes to write his
gospel, therefore, he goes straight to the heart of things. He
tells us that Jesus was/is God's spoken word; that he is a
statement from God; that he is a man and a message that
must be heard. He paints an opening picture with powerful
broad strokes. He is re-echoing and rewording the message
of the Baptist: 'This is it! He has come. It has happened as
promised.' The words tumble over one another as he speaks,
because, if ever words were anointed and inspired by God's
Spirit, these certainly are. John concludes his gospel by
telling us that, not only has the messenger come, but if everything that happened when he came was all written down,
'the whole world, I believe, could not contain the books that
could be written'.

Jesus tells us that to know him is to know the Father, to see
him is to see the Father, and to hear him is to listen to the
Father. In other words, Jesus is the Father's final and definitive word. There is no more to be said. Jesus also said that his
words to us would judge us, because if he had not come and
spoken to us, we would have an excuse for our sins. We will
look at those words, and listen to them again, many many
times throughout this book.

3 The Teacher

We are all familiar with movies about a new discovery, and about the thinking and theses of the person who made the discovery. Such people move us all forward, even if only a little. Life is a journey. If I am not moving forward, then be sure I am moving backward. Life is dynamic, it is never static. 'Lord, I confess that my life is not all that it ought to be, but I thank you that it's a bit better than it used to be', is one of my favourite prayers. It is a good and necessary feeling to know that I am moving forward. The teacher is always in the business of discovery, of revelation, of moving forward. The teacher who is no longer learning something new, is no longer capable of being a good teacher. In the most impoverished countries in the world, the immediate priority is to feed them, but the long-term goal must be to educate them. 'If you want to feed me today, give me rice. If you want to feed me for the rest of my life, teach me how to grow rice.'

The teacher is one who brings another from the known to the unknown. In other words, what is known is the starting point. Jesus was a brilliant teacher. He began with sheep, birds of the air, fish, nets, shepherds, etc. He could point to these as he spoke. His starting point was the very core of their lives and their experience. Genuine teaching is an expression of love, which involves meeting and accepting the other where that person is. Because I myself spent most of my years in the teaching profession, I can claim to know a little about the subject. In the early days of our training, there was a general acceptance that a highly intelligent person would not make a good teacher, except, of course, with highly intelli-

gent pupils. I'm just stating what was our considered opinion
at that time, rather than asserting a fact! The implication was,
that to effectively impart information, it was necessary to
look through the eyes of the learners, and endeavour to see
the material from their perspective as well. Proper teaching
requires constant empathy, which provides the batteries for
the necessary patience! Personally, I would rephrase the
comment from our training college days to read: Highly
intellectual people do not make good teachers. There is a vast
difference between being intellectual, and being intelligent.
The intellectual has a tendancy to complicate, over-state, and
verbalise, while the really intelligent should be able to state
the most profound truths in simple everyday language.
Kirkegard said to Hegel, 'We philosophers are extraordinary
geniuses. By the time we have put words on a concept, you
can be sure that most people won't have an idea what we're
talking about. I met another philosopher in Copenhagen last
week, and when I asked him for directions to a street not far
away, he gave me a map of Europe!'

Let's get back to Jesus, before I convict myself as an intellectual! It is absolutely extraordinary the emphasis Jesus
placed on teaching. In the Acts of the Apostles, we are told
that 'Jesus came to do and to teach'. That's an interesting insight, because it says that he was prepared to do the thing
himself first, before teaching others what to do. A simple and
obvious example of that is when he washed the feet of the
disciples, and then asked them to do as he did. The whole
concept of incarnation is an overwhelming declaration of love,
acceptance, and forgiveness. All Jesus' teaching is spoken
against that background. 'In this is love', says John, 'not that
we love God, but that God first loved us. Little children, let us
love one another, because God first loved us.' That is God's
greatest teaching, and Jesus came in person to teach it. As I
said in chapter one, he is God's word of love. 'For God so
loved the world that he gave his only-begotten Son, so those
who believe in him may have everlasting life.'

I am always fascinated by the importance Jesus gave to teaching in his ministry. The crowds had been with him for a long time, they had come from afar, they were tired and hungry. 'Jesus had pity on them and he sat down and began to teach them.' That would be ridiculous in any other context! It is worth noting that it is the apostles, and no one else, not Jesus, not the crowd, who drew attention to the fact that the crowds were hungry and tired. Jesus knew their real hunger, and he had earlier declared 'not on bread alone do we live, but on every word that comes from the mouth of God'. In this, as in many other ways, Jesus is a sign of contradiction. It is is said that the greatest hunger on earth is not for bodily food, and I believe that to be true. If food could make us happy, then every well-fed person should be happy! The greatest teaching of Jesus was his own life. 'Learn from me' he tells us. His every word and action teaches us something. He has been studied, discussed, and written about for centuries, and, yet here is one more book. Not the final and definitive word, I hasten to add!

There are a few of what we might now call lengthy discourses (long sermons?) in the gospels. The Sermon on the Mount is a classic, and it contains a wealth of teaching on the mind-set and thinking of God. 'I never say anything unless the Father tells me to. They who hear me hear the Father.' The Eight Beautitudes present a whole way of living, of thinking, and of being. As a teacher, they give me a simple, direct, and definite set of teachings. I can begin with the conviction that, even if they don't practise them, my listeners can identify with the ideas of gentleness, meekness, detachment, honesty, and peace-making. I don't need to use those actual words, of course, because it is in the concept I am interested. We all know gentle folk who have something very special about them. We may not be able to put it into words, but, for example, in the case of Mahatma Ghandi or Martin Luther King, we cannot deny the strength and power of their meekness and gentleness. Every nation has at least one person who

stands out as being a powerful advocate for peace, even
when such a stance is very unpopular. We are all aware of
prisoners of conscience, and of the fate of those who took a
stand on the side of justice and fairplay. What I'm saying here
is that the material for writing the Eight Beautitudes can be
found in most of our morning newspapers! Genius is the ability to discern the obvious! The ways of God are not ours, and
we have to become open to seeing things his way, before we
come to see anything. I am every person in the gospels. I have
my own deafness, my own dumbness, my own blindness.
The gospels give us a very clear insight into the mind of God,
and the teachings of the gospels give us a very definite blue-
print for living.

Teaching is a two-way process between teacher and pupil.
If only one side is functioning, there is nothing happening.
The greatest teacher in the world cannot force, and would
never force, knowledge on an unwilling listener. Part of being
a good teacher is to awaken in the pupil a desire and willingness to learn, even to the point of having a real love of learning. It is significant that the apostles asked, 'Lord, teach us to
pray.' They had watched Jesus multiplying the loaves, healing the lepers, raising the dead, and yet it must have been
how he prayed that impresed them most. Jesus often spoke of
the inner hunger and thirst that we all have, and he invites all
to come to him. It is very easy to imagine Jesus standing on
the side of a mountain, with large crowds around him as he
spoke. They had come to listen to his teaching. At other times
he pulled out from the shore in a boat, and taught them from
there. His classroom was the world, it was any place where
people were gathered. And, frequently, this was the Temple.

From my own experience in the classroom, I am very
familiar with the idea of there being a certain identifiable
spirit in a school, or among a particular class, be that good or
bad. To sit at the feet of Jesus must have been a very powerful
and power-filled experience. His words were alive and life-
giving. *Theos* is the Greek for God, from which we have the

word enthusiasm, which literally means to have God within. Jesus must have been a wonderful enthusiastic teacher. We have all come across someone (a rarity!) of whom it is said, 'I could sit and listen to her/him all day.' Their enthusiasm is magnetic. Generally this comes from a deep-rooted belief in the truths they are presenting. The first requirement for being a good homilist is that the speaker believe the message being presented!

It is obvious that Jesus was a man with a mission. He was on fire with zeal for that mission, 'and how can I be at peace until it is accomplished?' His very meat, that which kept him alive, was to do the work of him who sent him. He was sent with a simple message, and he spoke it in our language. By doing, and following that by teaching, it became what is known in educational language as 'an object lesson.' By beginning where they were at, and pointing to things they owned, and situations they knew, he could bring them on a journey of discovery and revelation. I can readily understand the disciples on the road to Emmaus. Our ability to be alert, to be in touch, to be aware of what is happening around us, is directly effected by how things are within us. At the beginning, they were despondent and depressed. Jesus zeroed in on where they were, and why they were so. He then proceeded to lead them from there into a whole new discovery. Eventually 'their eyes were opened', and they remarked to each other, 'were not our hearts burning within us when he spoke, and when he explained the scriptures to us?'

There is a progression in such teaching. It begins with information. This is the basis. It has to do with teaching the core message of the gospel. It never ceases to amaze me how a generation like my own grew up with definitions, commandments, precepts, laws, rules, etc, and with very little awareness of the centrality of the gospel. In our religion classes we had copies of catechisms, Hart's *Christian Doctrine*, Sheehan's *Apologetics*, etc, etc, everything except a copy of the gospels! If I may be so presumptuous, I think I know why that was so.

Religion and church had taken over the running of things many years earlier, and very soon the Holy Spirit was redundant. When I was growing up, he was even called the Holy Ghost, which implied a very insubstantive reality. He was called in on the job once in a life-time, at Confirmation, but was then removed to the back-burner, unless needed at a later date for ordination.

It is very significant to see how Jesus' teaching began. He was anointed by the Holy Spirit, he was led by the Spirit into the Temple, and he spoke these famous words, 'The Spirit of the Lord is upon me. He has anointed me to bring good news to the poor; to proclaim liberty to captives, and to give new sight to the blind; to free the oppressed, and announce the Lord's year of mercy.' We speak here of the very core of evangelising. The Father sends Jesus, and the Spirit does the anointing, and opens up the heart pores of both speaker and the listener.

Words, in themselves, are but a collection of letters of the alphabet. They can have many meanings, depending on the spirit with which they are spoken. Sometimes I meet another who asks me how I am, and I don't really answer the question! Another could ask me the very same question, and I might spend several minutes by way of reply. The exact same words, spoken with a totally different spirit. Prayer is like that. I can, of course, say prayers, just as I could teach a parrot to say a prayer. I cannot, however, pray unless the Spirit of God is in my words. On a few occasions, when Jesus prayed out loud, we are told that 'he was filled with the joy of the Holy Spirit, as he exclaimed ....'

Enthusiam is contagious. It is a wonderful experience to sit in front of a teacher who is fully enthusiastic about the value and importance of what is being taught. Just as it is accepted that 'the noisy teacher makes a noisy class', so is it that the teacher who is bored, very quickly becomes boring. Jesus spoke of himself 'being on fire with a mission'. He said that he came 'to set fire to the earth'. Without wishing to be banal, might I suggest that Jeus saw himself as a salesman, with a product that everybody vitally needed, and he was fired up to awaken them to an awareness of that fact.

I like walking. I love walking in the country, along the base of mountains, or along the seashore. It is at times like that that I am often struck with how asleep we all can be. The church's liturgies, leading up to Christmas, call on us to 'wake up from your slumber, arise from your sleep'. It is amazing how much of any one of us can be lying dormant. It must be one of life's greatest tragedies, when someone drifts through life, not fully awake, and not too involved in what's going on. They take everything for granted. It is said that if you want to really appreciate something, have it stolen, get it back, and it then becomes very special.

I myself can think of teachers I had in school, and it was years later before I realised just how good they were. Artists fascinate me. I have a very good friend who is a painter. I love walking in the woods, or by the sea with her, because she gets so excited about the beauty, the colours, the textures, and the layers and layers of life that I myself would never see. I remember sharing space with a poet a few years ago. I was working in a nursing home, and he was convalescing there. After breakfast he went for a stroll along by the harbour. I will never forget the expression on his face, and the spark in his eye as he returned, filled with awe and delight at what he had seen that morning. Jesus speaks on several occasions about the need to stay awake. He speaks of being alert, of being ready, of watching (as we pray). He tells stories of foolish virgins, and of workmen who were not ready when the bridegroom or the king arrived. I sometimes think of this alertness being the equivalent of wearing an antenna on our heads. God is always present, is always speaking, is always involved.

There is a television set quite close to where I am writing, but the screen is blank. There is a radio on the window right beside me. I like silence when I write, so both mediums of communication are switched off. This means that all those people out there, acting in front of cameras, or speaking into microphones, are wasting their sweetness on the desert air, as far as I am concerned! Communication has to be at least two-way, or it is no-way.

Jesus taught with authority. This literally means that he spoke the word, the message, of the author. He never said anything unless the Father told him to do so. His listeners re-marked that they had never heard anyone speak with such authority. He declares that he knows what he is speaking about. In John's gospel, he speaks at great length about the Bread of Life. Some of his listeners thought that this teaching was too difficult to accept, so 'they walked away, and walked no more with him'. He didn't run after them, he didn't offer to change or water-down the message. He had spoken his truth, and he left them with the straight choice of accepting or rejecting it.

Jesus came 'for the fall as well as for the resurrection of many'. There is nothing automatic about it. If his listeners were not free to walk away, they were not free to stay. Later on, he would tell his apostles to speak their truth and, if that was not accepted, they should shake the dust of that town from their feet, and move on elsewhere. Teaching is a service, and it must never become tyrannical, nor should it become brain-washing. The response from the listener must be vol-untary, and personal. It is only when the information is freely accepted that it can lead to formation and, eventually, to transformation. The gospel message is invitation, with a very definite RSVP attached. 'Let your yes be yes, and your no be no ... You are either for me, or against me.' Not to respond is itself a response. The opposite to love is not hatred, but indif-ference.

The teaching process has two dimensions to it, i.e. the message and the response. By any standards, Jesus was the most brilliant and gifted teacher who ever spoke. There is not one *maybe* or one *might* in the whole gospel. His message is crystal clear, and he thanks the Father for presenting, through him, a message that is so simple that the intellectual and worldly-wise would fail to recognise its profondity, and dismiss it as the demented ramblings of a fool and a dreamer. But, as with the child who clearly saw that 'the king has no clothes', the message makes total sense, and is not at all complicated to those who have the heart of a child, whose mind and heart are not yet complicated.

God has no grandchildren. In God's eyes, each of us is a simple child, despite the attempts of the world, of age, and of life, to complicate that simple truth. The message was first spoken through the very appearance of a child among us at Bethlehem. It began in total simplicity, and it continued that way. Through his very presence, as well as through every word he spoke, and everything he did, Jesus was revealing the Father, and that is the most profound message ever spoken to the human heart.

4 The Healer

Whenever we think of the results of original sin, we speak of so much more than just sin. We must also speak of a sinful condition that leaves us with human brokenness, and the many results of that original Fall. As humans, we are made of clay, 'and onto clay we shall return'. God breathed his Spirit into the clay, and we became alive. As a result of original sin, that creation of God became polluted, and another spirit predominated. The only way back for us is re-creation. Jesus came to remove what was evil, and to restore what was good. 'I came that you should have life, and have it more abundantly'. He came to lead us back from alienation, from death, from sickness, into friendship, to life, and to health.

Jesus himself was God's healing word, he was God's healing touch. The Father reached out to us through him, to make us whole again. What God created was good. As Jesus explained about the weeds among the wheat, 'an enemy has done this'. It is just not possible for us to re-create ourselves, to lift ourselves out of the quicksand of our sinful condition. In himself, Jesus took on our human condition, so that 'he who was without sin became sin, … and through his wounds we are healed.' The absence of well-being within our spirits was reflected in the outward condition of our bodies. Blindness can be so much more than a physical handicap. There is a deafness of heart, and a crippling spirit that can choke the spark of life within. Jesus came as a human being. Therefore, it was through the human in us that he would heal. As he healed the eyes of the body, he would also open the eyes of the soul. He would heal both body and soul. He would heal totally, or not at all. I couldn't imagine him healing a blind man, and then have that man go down the road full of hatred for his brother. That could not be called healing in any true sense of that word. 'And the man followed Jesus down the road, praising and glorifying God.'

Jesus did not go around healing anybody. He went around with the power to heal, and the person on the roadside had to make a decision. God doesn't give me anything; he offers me everything. Bartimeus, the blind man, had a choice. He sensed the excitement, and he asked what was happening. He was told that 'Jesus of Nazareth was passing by'. The choice facing Bartimeus was to stop Jesus and be healed, or die a blind man. Jesus was passing by and he would have kept on going, if Bartimeus allowed that happen. He did not allow that happen, however. He seized the moment of grace, and he cried out with all his heart, 'Jesus, son of David, have mercy on me.' The people around him tried to silence him, but he shouted all the louder, 'Son of David, have mercy on me.' It is not possible for a human being to fall on his knees, cry out to God, and not be heard. Jesus stopped, and called Bartimeus to come to him.

In a way this was strange. Bartimeus was blind, and Jesus might well have been expected to go over to him. No, the onus is still on Bartimeus, the initiative is still his. Bartimeus flung off his old cloak, and ran towards Jesus. Then another strange thing happened. Jesus spoke to him, and asked, 'What do you want me to do for you?' Now it must have been obvious to everyone present that the man was blind. Surely he wanted to see again. Perhaps, but he had to say so himself. Of course, God knows what's wrong with us, and yet Jesus says, 'Ask and you will receive.' And so Bartimeus was brought to the final requirement for being healed, i.e. he told Jesus exactly what was wrong, and he asked Jesus to heal him.

In a general way, it could be said that there were certain conditions needed for a miracle in the gospel. The first was the total failure of all the efforts and attempts of the persons themselves to solve their own problems. The little woman in the crowd had spent every penny she had over the previous twelve years, and was still not any better. The man at the pool had been there for thirty-three years, and he still was waiting for a healing. Peter had fished all night and caught nothing. I'm sure he tried every method, and he probably rowed to every corner of the lake, before conceding defeat. It is reasonable to presume that Jairus had done everything possible for his daughter, and it was only when he realised that all his best was just not enough, that he came to Jesus. It is obvious that the centurion held his servant in very high regard, and was prepared to go to any lengths to ensure his well-being. From the story it would seem that he himself ran off to meet Jesus, leaving the others looking after the servant. When the miracle happened, it was they who came running to the centurion to announce the good news.

I find it totally absorbing, insightful, and fascinating to 'watch' Jesus healing. It tells so much about him, and it explains so much of what he brought to his mission. He is obviously not going to do for us something we can easily do for ourselves. (Like the old man, whose beard went on fire, and he prayed it might start raining!) In our own day, I see the Lord continuing his healing ministry at the hands of the medical and the caring profession. However, there comes a line where the human runs out of resources, and God himself has to intervene directly. That, I think, is what we call a miracle. Only God can work miracles. We ourselves, of course, can have a very real say in providing the conditions for the miracle. Our contribution is called *faith*.

Let us look at faith for a few minutes, and try to grasp the concept, and look at the reality. Faith is a response to love. There are people I cannot trust, because I have no reason to believe that they care too much about me, or about my welfare. Convince me that they love me, and that they have my best interests at heart, and then, and only then, should you ask me to trust them. Trust and lack of trust plays a major role in our lives. Someone who is struggling with an addiction or a compulsion can well end up not being able to trust themselves. They have damaged themselves, and everybody and everything belonging to them, so much over the years, that, of all the people on this earth, the one they can trust least is themselves. Nowadays, we speak of subliminal effects, and what happens when a message is repeated again and again into the brain. My reason for saying that is that it might be so much easier for us to grasp the whole concept of faith if we had an inner voice that kept repeating *God is love*. That simple, but profound, truth is the backdrop to the whole gospel story. In simple English, if I can grasp and accept that basic simple truth, I'm right. Jesus said that no one knows the Father except the Son, and those to whom the Son chooses to reveal him. 'Lord Jesus, please reveal the Father's love to me.' The saint is not the person who loves God, but the one who is totally convinced that God loves her.

Faith is the proper response to love. Jesus really loves me, therefore, I trust him to do what's best for me, and I can turn to him with total confidence and expectation. Once again, we find ourselves with the two components of salvation, i.e. what Jesus has done, and how I am prepared to avail of that. Many of the people in the gospel fill me with amazement. We speak today about the importance of being Christian, and how central it is that we live and move in the Spirit if we are to be open to the truths of the gospel. Many of these people, however, were pagans, illiterate, outcasts, 'nobodies'. And yet from their hearts came a cry that caused God to stop and listen. I can only reflect on what I think may have happened here. They had run out of human resources, they were totally bereft of everything, and, when I'm on the broad of my back, there's only way to look, and that's up. Even before healing them, the very presence of Jesus generated some new sense of aliveness and of hope. They had every reason in the world to be in the depths of despair, without a hope or without a prayer. And yet, once they saw Jesus, a whole new hope was awakened in them.

I repeat the word *hope* here very deliberately, because when I let go of that, I have crossed that line of no-return, and there's no way back. Hope is always the mark of the Christian, and Peter tells us to 'always have an explanation to give those who ask you the reason for the hope that you have.' Because the Spirit the Father gives us will never leave us, it is relatively easy for the Christian to hold on to the hope that 'all is well, all will be well, and all manner of things will be well.'

The only way I can figure out many of the situations in the gospel is by reflecting what it must have felt like to be in the presence of Jesus, and to try to imagine what was going on in the hearts of those who stopped him. The leper had nowhere to go, no way to turn, no place to hide. He was beaten, mentally as well as physically. It might have been years since he saw love in another's eyes, or a smile on another's face. His world was one of darkness and hopelessness. And then one day Jesus walked into his world, into his darkness. I can only imagine what that was like. I am not sure whether my eyes would be riveted on the leper or on Jesus. On reflection, I think I would look at Jesus first, because whatever came from him, through his look, and through his very presence, was what sparked whatever happened in the leper. The extremes had met. Without a positive and a negative, there would be no power in a wall-socket.

We have many instances in the gospel where there is special reference to how Jesus looked at people. For example, when he met Peter, he looked at him before he spoke. He would look at Peter on a later occasion, when Peter had denied him. The look hadn't changed. It was still a look of love. Peter melted before that look, and the acceptance and love that it held, and 'going outside, he wept bitterly.' Jesus looked across the city of Jerusalem and he cried, because ' salvation was within your grasp, and you would not accept it.

So often I would have gathered you, as a hen gathers her chicks under her wings, but you would not.'

In several instances in the gospel, faith is a journey. Jesus said, 'If you love me, you will obey me, and then you can ask the Father for anything in my name, and you will receive it.' The ten lepers were not healed when he sent them on their journey of faith. They obeyed him, and 'on the way they were healed'. The centurion was sent on his journey and, as he made his way home, his servants came to tell him that the sick one was well again. Jesus travelled with Jairus and, even when word came that his daughter was dead, Jesus simply said, 'Just trust me.' In many ways, faith is a journey. It is a journey from the head to the heart, to the feet. In my head I may know that Jesus is God. That, however, is not faith. Even Satan knows that. That is no more than knowledge, or mental assent. When faith reaches my feet, like Peter, I am prepared to step over the side of the boat. When Peter kept his eyes on Jesus, he was able to walk on water. When his attention moved back to himself and his surroundings, he panicked, and began to sink.

Faith can be both virtue and gift. As a virtue, it is something I can practise, just like kindness. It is like a grain of mustard seed and, if nourished, nurtured, and developed, it can grow into a huge tree 'in which the birds of air can find shelter'. Many others can find help and support in my faith. One man was unconscious and he was lowered through the roof by his friends, right down to where Jesus was in the house. 'Jesus marvelled at their faith', and he healed the man. The couple and their guests at Cana benefited from the faith of Mary, as she approached Jesus. I learned to walk by walking, and to talk by talking. Similarly, if I exercise my faith, it will grow. In a way, I can come to know God in somewhat the same way I come to know any of those around me. By spending time with them, experiencing their presence, and becoming aware of their love and care, I also come to trust them. It is interesting to note that it was only to the apostles that, on more than one occasion, Jesus had to address the words, 'Why did you doubt, you of little faith?'

Faith is also a gift, one of the gifts of the Holy Spirit. There is a slight difference here. In this case faith is a *charism*, which is a word used to speak of a gift that is given to be used in the service of others. It is another expression of love. The Canaanite woman was hardly able to made subtle distinctions in matters of faith, but she loved her daughter deeply, and her love included all the gifts, being in itself the greatest gift of all.

The time came for Jesus to take leave of his apostles. He spoke of the Spirit who would come to lead them in his ways. He commissioned them to go and preach in his name. He then spoke those marvellous words, 'And these are the signs that shall accompany you. In my name you will ... lay hands on the sick, and they will be healed.' All of this is the gift of faith in action. In other words, if I go forth to do the work of the Lord, I should do so only in the conviction that wherever that may lead me, I will discover the necessary gift there. As needed, I will have access to the gifts of prophecy (speaking God's word), wisdom, discernment, knowledge, faith, miracles, etc. All of this goes with the job! It is part of the 'tool-kit' the Lord supplies to those who go forth in his name.

Faith begins with belief. You need your car serviced, you have never been in these parts before, and you ask me to recommend a garage. I suggest Mc Donald's, saying that they do a good job, and do not overcharge. You take me at my word, you believe, you act on that belief, and you bring your car to Mc Donald's. When you collect your car, you discover that they did a good job, and they did not overcharge. The next time you need your car serviced you act on faith, because now you know that it is the right thing to do. I'm sure many a person in the gospel came to Jesus on the word of another. They knew someone who was healed, they heard of someone who was healed. That was a good starting point. Something seemed to happen, however, once they came into the presence of Jesus. His presence touched something deep within, and the spark of faith was ignited. All this happened because of their own deep awareness of their own powerlessness, and their inability to solve or resolve their own situation. At the same time, and in that same place, there were religious leaders, and they were so full of their own self-righteousness that there was no room within for anything to happen. This is chilling to reflect on, when even Jesus was rendered powerless in the presence of such people. The openness has to come from us before God can enter. The door of our heart has but one handle, and it is on the inside. The only limits to what the Lord can do in my life are the ones I myself can set.

To be in touch with my own brokenness, and my need for healing, it can help if I see myself as being everybody in the gospel. I have my own blindness, my own deafness, my own demons; I am crippled in many ways by life, and I am tossed around in my own storms; I can experience the rottenness of my own leprosy, and the burdens of life can leave me in a high degree of emotional fever. When I stand before the Lord, what do I bring, what do I say, what do I hear? 'Do you believe that I can do this?' 'I believe, Lord, help my unbelief. Lord, increase my faith.' 'Your faith healed you. As you believe be it done onto you. Oh woman, great is your faith. When the Son of Man comes will he find any faith on this earth? The sin of this world is unbelief in me.' What priceless material for reflection and contemplation.

The gospel is now, and I am every person in the gospel. There is one very important question Jesus asked, to which I did not yet refer. He turned to the man at the pool, and he asked him, 'Do you want to be healed?' That is a loaded question. Without any great reflection, I would probably reply, 'Of course I want to be healed.' It's not as simple as that, however. The man had been sitting at the pool for thirty-eight years. One can get used to a way of living, after all that time. If he is healed, nothing is ever going to be the same again. Not only will he lose the pity of others, he will also have to let go of his own long-nourished self-pity. He may now have to work for a living. Is it posssible that some years down the road he could regret that he was healed? We all are familiar with the prayer of Augustine. 'Lord, make me chaste, but not yet.' The alcoholic may not want to give up alcohol. All he wants is some magic formula that will permit him continue the drinking without the negative effects. To such a one Jesus could well ask, 'Do you want to be healed?' It is important to remember that, should I approach Jesus in search of healing, the onus is not totally on him! I often think of God being on standby, waiting for me to get out of the way and let him move in!

5 The Provider

There is absolutely no order of priority involved in the titles for these reflections. When it comes to reflecting on the person and the teachings of Jesus, it matters little where we start. I myself find that all I need do is begin a reflection, and just see where it leads, or to what it may lead. The word *provider* is defined as a person dealing with all or many kinds of goods. To understand just how extraordinary a provider Jesus was, and continues to be, we need to have deep convictions about the reality of our own finiteness and limitations. No point in speaking of bread to someone moving away from the table after a sumptuous meal! Before I can have any hope of appreciating just how bounteous and generous Jesus is, I need to grow in awareness and acceptance of the details of my human condition.

I own nothing. Everything I have is on loan. One heart attack and it's all over! I was carried into a church one time, and I was not consulted, or too involved, as they baptised me. Sometime in the future, I'll be carried into a church again, and I won't be consulted or too involved this time either. To try to run the show in the meantime is nothing short of insane and irresponsible behaviour. Human nature, human life, and human existence is something extremely delicate and complicated. Life is so much bigger than any of us. It is said that the wise man is he who knows how much he doesn't know. Because of the way God has tied himself in with us, and with our destiny, we end up with the paradox that the less we have the more is available to us. If my fists are clenched, clinging to what I have, I am not free to accept whatever else is offered.

John the Baptist said that he had to decrease if Jesus were to increase. Paul speaks of rejoicing in his weakness, because 'when I am weak, then I am strong, because the power of God works best in weak people'. This is an extraordinary truth, and certainly flesh and blood could never accept, let alone reveal this. It is part of the wonderful mystery of God that we call the divine providence. Jesus spoke of the birds of the air, and the lilies of the field, and how his heavenly Father cared for them. I'm not suggesting it as a truth, but when I was a child growing up in the country, we were always sure if a severe winter was up ahead. The extra heavy crop of fruits and berries was accepted by the people as an example of God's provision for the birds in the months ahead.

Jesus came to provide. The greatest hunger on earth is the need to be loved, the need to belong. The invitation of Jesus was to nothing less than full membership within the family of God. In his first letter, John wrote, 'The Life made himself known, we have seen him, we are his witnesses, and we are telling you of Eternal Life. He was with the Father, and he appeared to us. We make known to you him whom we have seen and heard, that you may be in fellowship with us, with the Father, and with his Son, Jesus Christ.' Paul says that 'having given us Christ Jesus, will the Father not surely give us everything else?' There is no way that human intellect can possibly grasp the width and the depth of the providence of God. As with the wine at Cana, or the loaves and fishes, there is always much to spare when everybody has had their fill.

Cana was the scene of a most unusual miracle. The basic conditions for a miracle, mentioned in the last chapter, seem to be absent. There is no great hardship or deprivation referred to in the account, nor is there is anyone, except Mary, who has any idea that Jesus might be able to do anything about the situation. While not pretending to have any profound revelation about this, or any other part of the gospel, for that matter, I dare to offer an explanation. Jesus was now thirty years of age, and Mary had been close to him for most, if not all of that time. In a very undramatic, down-to-earth way, she had become the witness to an ongoing daily miracle. In her own eyes she was nothing, and in her own eyes she did nothing. She had long come to believe that if we let God have what we've got, miracles will follow, 'because nothing is impossible with God'. At Cana, the only thing they had in abundance was water. All that was needed was to make available what they had, and then 'do whatever he tells you to'. God becomes God in my life the very instant I get out of the way, and stop playing God.

Something similar happened with the loaves and fishes. We can understand the apostles' sense of hopelessness and futility when they present such a meagre meal, and ask 'What is this among so many?' That was all they had, and that was all that Jesus needed. Let him have them, get out of the way, and let him take over. It is often difficult in life to accept the fact that 'Whatever I have is enough, if I am willing to make that available to God.' Two of the Ten Commandments speak of 'coveting' something that is not mine, but belongs to another. To covet is to be avaricious, greedy, and to want what belongs to another. Just as there is never enough alcohol for the alcoholic, so there is never enough of anything for the greedy and the selfish. 'Why be like the pagans?' Jesus asks. 'They worry and concern themselves about such things. Your heavenly Father knows your needs, and he will supply everything you need, if you seek his kingdom, and the lifestyle that goes with it.'

Living in God's kingdom is about an attitude, not a geographical entity. If the world is my kingdom, then I will totally depend on worldly goods for my survival, my satisfaction, my gratification. The world provides its own false gods of money, power, wealth, pleasure, etc. To live in the world is to give myself totally to the pursuit and to the service of such false deities. The gods, of course, are false, and so what they offer and promise is also false, and can never deliver on their promises. There is an empty space within the heart of all

God's creatures, and nothing short of God himself can fill it. 'You have made us for yourself, O Lord, and our hearts can never be at rest until they rest in you,' is a well-known quote from Augustine.

To live in the kingdom of God, and according to the norms of that kingdom, is something entirely different. There is only one God here, and that God provides everything needed for living and dying in that kingdom. The kingdom now is called 'heaven' later on, so, in a real sense, heaven begins now, and the road to heaven is heaven. The atmosphere of God's kingdom, the very air I breathe for life, is called the Holy Spirit, the breath and power of God. That is the breath that was breathed into the clay at the time of creation, before the pollutants of sin, sickness, and death entered into the mix. 'Learn to live and to walk in the Spirit' is the advice of Paul. God's providence is seen at its highest when we are open to the possibility of living and walking in the power of God. In the eyes of Jesus, changing water into wine, or multiplying the loaves and fishes must have been quite insignificant in themselves. They did have a profound significance, of course, even if the recipients were unable to grasp that fact.

It is intriguing to watch Jesus effect some of his healings. I don't think it would have been essential to use mud and water to restore the sight of the blind man. I can only surmise that it had something to do with using the ordinary to move people to the extraordinary; like a teacher bringing a class from the known to the unknown. Again and again, we see Jesus make full use of what was available. Peter filled the boat with fish, but he had to use his nets. Jesus may not have been hungry, but by going to eat in the house of Zaccheus, he was using the meal as a symbol of acceptance, friendship, and salvation. Bartimeus could have held onto his old cloak, but, by throwing it aside as he ran to Jesus, he was letting go of the past, and coming into the healing of the present moment. He used bread at Emmaus as a very down-to-earth reminder of who he was, and, in that way 'their eyes were opened.' In speaking to the Samaritan woman at the well, he opened her heart to his teaching, and he based that teaching on the very water she had come to draw. When he was confronted with the Pharisees, and the woman taken in adultery, his actions are intriguing. He stooped down and wrote with his finger in the sand. Did he write something specific about any of his onlookers? Did he imply that our sins are written in sand, and are blown away by the breath of God's love? Was his action something deliberately trivial to bring the Pharisees down a peg? We don't know, but it still intrigues. In every sense of the word, Jesus was very down-to-earth.

When we consider Jesus as a provider, it would be wrong to limit ourselves to wine, to loaves, to fish. There are several examples of him providing loving and positive support. Larazus, Martha, and Mary were friends of his. No doubt, over the years, they had provided him with many of the necessities of life. Jesus loved Lazarus, and his sisters. It is reasonable to expect that he spent leisurely hours with them over the years. I have no doubt whatever that, wherever Jesus was, whoever he was with, whatever he was doing, he was giving to those around him. Of all the claims to recognition that little house in Bethany may have had, and still has, the greatest, of course, is that Jesus made it a place of rest, a retreat house. The householders could never have asked for anything more than that. And then Lazarus died. There are several strange aspects of this story. Jesus was told several days earlier that Lazarus was sick, and he was asked to come. Initially, it appeared he was headed straight for Bethany, and then, for whatever reason, he remained where he was for the following two days. It would appear that going to Bethany was to bring him very near to Jerusalem, and his disciples reminded him 'Master, the Jews wanted to stone you. Are you going there again?' From a human point of view, Jesus was in a bind. His friend was seriously ill and he wanted to be with him; but by going anywhere near Jerusalem, he was putting his life on the line. There were times when the Jews had attempted to kill him, but 'his time had not yet come.' 'Nobody takes my life from me', Jesus announced, 'I will lay it down, and I will take it up again'. He would, of course, go up to Jerusalem, but not until he was ready, and the hour had come. Throughout all of this time he carried his friend Lazarus in his heart. He referred to him several times during those days. 'This illness will not end in death; rather it is for God's glory, and the Son of God will be glorified through it.' As he moved towards Bethany he announced that 'Our friend Lazarus has fallen asleep, but I am going to waken him.' The apostles took his words literally, though Jesus meant that Lazarus had died. There were so many things happening around Jesus at that moment, that he must have experienced much inner anguish. His friend was dead, his friends Martha and Mary were bereaved, and he himself was coming very close to the completion of his mission. He met Martha and Mary, shared their grief with them, wept with them, accepted them as they were, and then he turned to the Father from whom all life comes, and he asked that the gift of life be restored to Lazarus. He even involved those around in the process. When Lazarus woke from the sleep of death, he was wrapped from head to toe in bandages, and might well have smothered. Jesus turned to those around him with the words, 'Unbind him, and let him go.' It is ironic that the excitement generated by the story of Lazarus galvanised the Jewish leaders into making one final push against Jesus. Lazarus still had to die again, of course, at a later date but, for the present, Jesus provided the support, the hope and the life that was needed at that time.

We cannot speak of Jesus as a provider, of course, without reflecting on his greatest provision of all, i.e. giving us himself as food and drink for the journey of life. Life is a journey. The journery of the Hebrews out of bondage in Egypt, through the desert, into the Promised Land, that is the model for all of our journeys. Moses for them, is Jesus for us. The journey through the desert is a saga of how God cared for them, protected them, provided for them. They were invited to undertake a walk of faith, a pilgrimage towards the place where God dwelt. This journey, with very significant changes, is a very accurate replica of our own journey. Jesus is our Moses, leading us out of the bondage of sin, sickness, and death, through the struggles of life, and into the Father's home, which, for us, is the Promised Land. Jesus himself is the manna. 'They who eat my body, and drink my blood have everlasting life, and I will raise them up on the last day, for my flesh is food indeed, and my blood is drink indeed. Your fathers ate manna in the desert, and they died. Anyone who eats this bread will live forever ...'

Moses had many problems with the people he led. They were always complaining. God gave them bread, so they complained they had no water. God instructed Moses to strike a rock with his stick, and water flowed from the rock. (Incidently, Moses didn't fully trust God, so he made doubly sure by striking the rock a few times! He was punished for this by not being allowed actually enter the Promised Land, even if it was within sight.) Jesus pointed to himself, and announced, 'Anyone who is thirsty, let that person come to me.' He spoke to the woman at the well about the water he could provide that would take away thirst altogether, becoming a perpetual spring within her, giving her eternal life. This is very powerful figurative language. He had already turned water into wine, and now he offered an even greater miracle. Beneath the driest desert there is plenty of water, but it just cannot make it to the surface. Jesus speaks of the Holy Spirit being a fountain of living water rising up within a person.

In all of this Jesus was saying, yet again, something that was central to his message: 'I am the Way, and no one comes to the Father in any other way.' There is no way back from bondage and slavery, through the desert of life, into the Promised Land, except through Jesus. He is the food, the drink, the life, the redeemer, the saviour, the Lord. His provision is total. The Father had entrusted everything to him, and even when the Spirit comes '... he will not be presenting his own ideas; he will be telling you what he has heard ... He will bring me glory by revealing to you whatever he receives from me. All that the Father has is mine; this is what I mean when I say that the Spirit will reveal to you whatever he receives from me.' This is what Paul means when he says that 'having given us Christ Jesus, will the Father not surely give us everything else?' In Jesus we have everything. Jesus is the provider no matter what the need; he is the answer, no matter what the question.

6 The Mystic

Jesus is like a many-sided prism. No matter from which angle you look, you always see something new. Because he is both God and man, he is everything in himself. He is totally human, while being profoundly mystical. A mystic is someone who seeks through contemplation and self-surrender to obtain union with the divine; someone who believes in spiritual apprehension of truths beyond our human understanding. I believe that Jesus was both God and man, but I'm not sure that he himself was always aware of that fact. Using our humanity as his base, and with the openness of the pure of heart, he journeyed towards the experience of the deity. I believe this journey to be possible to anyone who is redeemed from bondage, who is not weighed down and held back by human weaknessess, and all the burden of our fears, anxieties, guilts, and selfishness. Jesus certainly encountered all of this. 'He was like us in all things but sin … He was tempted in everyway like we are, but did not sin', Paul tells us.

I think of Jesus as suffering enormously from loneliness. This was not just because he was among us as an exile, removed from his Father's home. Effectively, the Father's home is everywhere, so that would not have been the problem. The loneliness he would have experienced would have been 'the loneliness of the long-distance runner'. Deaf people must often be lonely, because communication is a lifeline for most of us. Hence the phenomenal growth in telecommunications. Giant steps are being made to facilitate communication, possibly at the risk that everybody ends up communicating, and there's nobody listening anymore! Mary was a unique and

very special human being. She was the only person on this
earth who could enter Jesus' world and, somehow, understand. It is significant that she was not blinded by the myopia
of original sin and selfishness. 'Blessed are the pure of heart,
they shall see God.' The world of Jesus had no boundaries,
with an infinity of possibilities. He came that we should have
life and have it to the full. It is reasonable, therefore, to expect
that he himself was totally alive, and fully vibrant. As he
walked the countryside, he would have been completely
alert, to see and hear things that his companions, preoccu-
pied in their own little world, would have totally missed.

Life has brought me into personal contact with a few
artists and a few poets. I thoroughly enjoy their company, because of their heightened awareness. I spoke in an earlier
chapter of how I often ask myself: How asleep am I? It is
scary at times to become aware of the areas of one's being
that are dormant and non-productive. The mystic is involved
with mystery and awe, and there is a constant sense of discovery and of revelation. The very word 'revelation' comes
from the Latin *re-velare*, or the French *reveiller*, which implies
wakening up. From this we get our word *vigil*, which involves
being on the alert. It is significant that on the Mount of
Transfiguration or in the Garden of Gethsemane, Jesus had to
waken up his apostles, who kept falling asleep. I don't believe that God wants us to be deprived of sleep, at least that
much sleep needed to function in a healthy way. What I do
believe, however, is that, when not actually asleep, we should
be awake!

Again and again in the gospels there is reference to Jesus
going off to be alone, and spending all of the night in prayer. I
wouldn't dare intrude on the sacredness of such moments,
but I can see a great deal of purpose in all of this. Jesus never
said anything unless the Father told him. It was necessary,
therefore, that he listen to the Father, so as to have a message
to pass on. At such times he opened his heart to be charged
with the energy of the Father's love. With his humanity

alone, he could never have kept going. He had put aside his
own divinity, but, like any of us, he still had full access to the
divine. He had joined us on our side of the Red Sea, but he
kept his mind and his heart focused on the Promised Land.
His going aside at night-time was to strengthen that umbili-
cal cord with the source of his life. 'My very food is to do the
will of him who sent me.' Jesus had no other reason for being
on this earth than to fulfil the mission entrusted to him by the
Father. It is not too far-fetched to imagine the vast amount of
time spent by a country's ambassador being in touch with the
home country. It might well be the first thing to be done each
morning, and the last thing at night. It is central that a life
have a purpose, and not become some sort of meandering,
meaningless existence. Jesus was a man with a mission, a person fully enthused with zeal for that mission.

We are all familiar with the concept of getting away for a
while 'to take time out, to have some time for ourselves'. In
very non-theological language, these night sessions were
Jesus' lifeline to sanity. The gospels are replete with his message being questioned, his word being misinterpreted, his
mission under threat of being hijacked. In this was the loneliness. Others insisted on trying to make him become something that he wasn't, and that he never wanted to be.
Misunderstanding can be acceptable and excusable, but the
deliberate attempts of the religious leaders to twist what he
said, to hear only what they wanted to hear, and to be completely deaf to the simplicity of the message being offered; all
of this must have brought endless frustration, and deep personal loneliness. As someone who could heal the deaf, and
restore sight to the blind, it must have been deeply offensive
to meet so many who were determined neither to hear nor to
see.

I have studied the paintings of several artists of their
impression of Jesus alone at prayer. I like most of them, probably because anything that helps me visualise what it might
have been like is welcome. No artist would ever attempt to

capture what was really going on, of course, because that was
of a depth and a width that was so much greater than any
canvas. It was a question of absorption, of being totally en-
veloped by the awe of the divine. Every sense, every pore,
every extremity is open, alert, and fully tuned-in. Jesus is at
home here, and he feels at home here. This was his time to report back, to reflect and, above all, to listen. His whole purpose was to do the will of the one who sent him. He never
said anything unless the Father told him. His faithfulness to
the Father's will was infinitely more important than any
human successes or failures he might have with his followers
the next day. He would accept full responsibility for his role,
and the others would have to do likewise. Later he told his
apostles, 'If they do not listen to you, shake the dust of their
town from your feet, and move on ...'

We speak of the Father, Son, and Spirit as the Trinity, three
persons in one God. I can have a cup of water, a snowball, or
a bowl of hailstones, and yet all I have is water in different dimensions. The whole story of redemption involves each
member of the Trinity. The Father initiates it, as it were, when
he sends Jesus. Jesus carries out the plan, and the Spirit
comes to complete it. It is not possible, of course, to point to a
particular moment, and say, 'Here's where the programme
for our redemption began', but there is one very significant
moment that must surely be a high-point in the process. Jesus
went to the Jordon to be baptised by John the Baptist. This
caused a strong reaction in John, who knew, of course, that
Jesus didn't belong in the kind of people who flocked out to
him. John couldn't understand, of course, that Jesus was
coming here on behalf of all sinners, because he had come to
take away the sins of the world. Jesus was not, as it were, fly-
ing solo in what he was doing. He was never alone, even
though, on the cross, he had a very real sense of aloneness
and loneliness. As he came up out of the waters of the Jordon,
the Spirit was seen to come upon him in visible form, and the
Father's voice was heard to call out, 'This is my beloved Son

in whom I am well pleased. Listen to him.' In other words, they were in this together. Jesus was the hand of God stretched out to sinners, held out in welcome, and in friend-ship. It was necessary then, for Jesus to be in constant contact with the Father and the Spirit so that together they might complete the plan.

Using human language, with all its limitations, it is as if Jesus were on his own for the first thirty years. He did his own personal novitiate as a human being. He had walked the walk, before attempting to talk the talk. He experienced what it was to be 'like us in all things but sin.' His human experi-ence was totally human, and not some sort of masquerade or pretence. In fact, he was so ordinary that, later on, when signs and miracles began to accompany him, his neighbours and acquaintances of many years were absolutely amazed. It is not too far-fetched to suggest that it was during those years that he himself discovered his origins, his potential, and his mission. After all, surely alot of this happens to all of us as we travel the journey of life. How many people set out on the journey, already in possession of all the answers? Life is a mystery, and it unfolds at each turn of the road. I can easily imagine Jesus' life being one of constant discovery, discovery about who God is, about who he is, and about who we are. As a child I often thought of those thirty years being a total waste of precious time, that could have been put to much bet-ter use! Obviously, I don't think that way any longer. I now see those years as the foundation on which was built all that was to follow.

In simple words, after thirty years of living, listening, and reflecting, Jesus knew all he needed to know to be able to begin his mission. From his very infancy he had travelled the Hebrew journey back from Egypt. It is significant that, while still a child, he actually travelled that journey back from Egypt. He had seen enough of oppression, possession, and depression to believe that these people needed a saviour. It was evident to him that humanity did not have within itself what could redeem it, and it was fidelity to the Father, and a profound determination to obey the Father in all things, that persuaded him to accept the role of Redeemer and Saviour. Knowing our condition, and all the ramifications involved in becoming entangled with human beings, he knew it would cost him everything. He also knew, however, that he could trust the Father totally. The original sin was one of disobedience, and it could only be set right by a supreme act of obedience.

The mystic has no horizons. The mind, the heart, and the soul become as big as the great outdoors. It is like looking at the earth from a space-shuttle, where everything becomes relative to what we have known till now. Contemplation is exploration, and reflection is prayer. Jesus arrived at a point where there were no barriers, no partitions, no divisions. He could look to one side and see humanity exactly as it is. He could turn towards God and see the deity in relationship to the universe. This is the goal of the mystic, the way of the hermit, and Jesus had arrived. He was in that unique go-between place where he could stretch out one hand to the Father, and the other to me. His role was to bring both hands together, resulting in the eternal union of the Father with his children. He passed on to us everything the Father told him. He assured us that there was no hidden agenda. 'They who hear me, hear the Father; they who see me, see the Father.'

Grief is the price we pay for love. If I don't want to cry at a funeral, then I should refrain from loving anyone. Jesus had an extraordinary capacity for love, and, therefore, he had every reason to cry. We know of times when he cried as he overlooked Jerusalem, or when he visited the tomb of Lazarus. I certainly believe that he must surely have cried at night when he was alone with the Father. This may seem strange, but I believe it makes a great deal of sense. He never said anything unless the Father told him. I could imagine Jesus saying these, or similar words, 'Father, I told them the story of the Prodigal Son, but they don't believe me. They're still afraid to come back to the garden. I told them the story about the Pharisee and the Publican, but they still cling to the letter of the law, and they equate goodness with observance of the law. I told them about the birds of the air, and the lilies of the field, but they continue to worry as much as any of the pagans. Father, they don't believe a word I tell them.' No wonder Jesus said 'The sin of this world is unbelief in me', and 'When the Son of Man comes, will he find any faith on this earth?'

I can see ways in which the mystic can be a lonely person, but I can see many ways and many reasons why the mystic should also be fully human and fully alive, with a vibrancy that is impossible to the burdened. The cage door is open, as it were, and the lark can soar, the seagull can glide. Many of us spend much of our lives in prisons of our own making. Some people who are severely physically limited may well feel themselves imprisoned in their bodies. A young woman who was totally immobile, with but a tiny movement in her big toe, with which she managed to press the keys of a specially constructed typewriter, wrote the following lines:

You ask me if I'm sad or bored,
or if my life it is abhorred;
and I tell you I am not,
that I can now accept my lot.
I remind your sadly-shaking head,
it's by body, not my mind, in bed.

Of such it is said that they are never less alone than when alone. Most of the loneliness Jesus experienced would have been in the middle of the pressing throngs. A couple can be in bed together, and yet be thousands of miles apart; while another couple could be many miles apart but experience a great closeness to each other.

There were times when Jesus wanted human company more than at other times. In Gethsemane, he wanted the comfort of the apostles' presence. He asked them to remain alert, to watch and pray. And yet they kept falling asleep on him.

The only one who was fully alert, beside Jesus, was Judas, because he had a personal investment in what was going on. It can be frightening at times when we glimpse human selfishness at close quarters. There is a sense of the obscene when we compare the openness of the mystic with the cunning alertness of the manipulator.

Jesus was human through and through. It was as if he left his humanity to one side for the present. Because of what he did with his humanity, and because of his total openness to the divine, is it possible that he could have raised his humanity to the level of the divine, being totally absorbed into it? The only limits to his life and his living were imagined by those around him. They were always ready and willing to pull him down, and to remind him of his humble origins in Nazareth.

The mystic is able to lift his eyes to the mountain, to see above and beyond the boundaries, to hear things not possible for the human ear. Yes, indeed, Jesus was alone. That was the pain in his cry on Calvary, 'My God, my God, why have you forsaken me?' At that moment, it appeared as if even the Father had deserted him, and he was totally alone.

Death is something I have to do. It is not something that another can do for me. Even if the room is filled with family and friends, the person in the bed has to face death alone. For one brief moment, Jesus experienced a sense of complete abandonment. It didn't last, because he was not abandoned. With his final breath, he offered his spirit into the Father's hands, and he bowed his head in obedience. The mystic had returned from his painful and lonely exile, and the process of resurrection for Jesus, and for all of us, was now to be completed.

7 The Exorcist

To get an overall backdrop to the story of salvation, it would help to read chapter twelve of the Book of Revelations. This is the very last book in the Bible (sometimes called the Apocalypse). These are considered to be a series of visions and messages received by St John, the apostle, towards the end of his life. Chapter twelve describes the expulsion of Lucifer from heaven. There was a battle in heaven. Lucifer refused to obey, and he did battle with the archangel Michael. Lucifer was defeated, and was expelled. What is very significant from our point of view is that we are told that Satan was 'cast down to earth'. This phrase is repeated four times in this one chapter. In other words, Satan is not in a place called 'hell'; he is alive and well, and living on this planet earth, and anywhere that he holds sway is hell.

The whole of chapter twelve is worth our consideration. It contains very powerful imagery. The woman is about to give birth and Satan is waiting to destroy the baby as soon as he is born. However, as soon as the baby is born, he is placed safely beyond the reach of Satan. This leads to the war in heaven. Tradition has it that the idea of submitting to someone who became a human being was too much for the proud one, who was called Lucifer (bearer of Light) before his expulsion, and whom we now call Satan (the enemy).

When Satan was cast down to earth, a voice was heard across the heavens proclaiming the triumph of those who remained faithful to God. They defeated Satan because of the redemption that Jesus was to bring, because of their testimony to that fact, and because of their willingness to live and die for that belief. In this is a wonderful example of one very important dimension of salvation history.

God cannot be 'boxed' into time. In other words, anything God does can actually effect everything that ever happened, and everything that will ever happen. What is *now* for God will also be *now* thousands of years hence. I am trying to avoid complication here, while not wishing to glide over the core truth. Let me put it this way. I remember watching the movie *Love Story*. At the beginning of the movie, we saw the young woman die, and then we were brought back through the whole story to reveal what went before. The end result is that she died, even though we spent an hour or two following what went on while she was still alive. The end result is that Satan is defeated, even if we spend our lives in the struggle against him. Satan will never ever admit defeat, and so he will battle on till the very last moment. If, however, you and I accept the fact that he is already defeated, then he can have no power over us.

The defeat of Satan is destined, as it were, from the moment of his expulsion, it is fully effected through the work and death of Jesus, and it is sucessfully completed through all of us who are willing to avail of the victory Jesus has earned for us. When Satan failed to destroy the child, he declared war on the woman. She too was placed by God beyond Satan's reach. This brought Satan to his final declaration of war: 'Then Satan became angry at the woman, and he declared war against the rest of her children – all who keep God's commandments, and confess that they belong to Jesus.' And now we can turn our attention to the part played by Jesus in this battle with Satan.

I remind myself again that Satan had been cast down to earth. When Jesus came he called Satan 'the prince of this world.' Satan brought Jesus to a high mountain, showed him all the kingdoms of this earth, and offered them to him if Jesus would adore him. In other words, all of this belonged to Satan, he was still running the show, and he knew why Jesus

had come. It is very significant that, at the very beginning of
Jesus' ministry, as soon as he came up out of the waters of the
river Jordan, he was led by the Spirit into the desert, where
Satan was waiting to take him on. The next stage of the battle
had begun. Satan would do everything within his power to
thwart the plans and the work of Jesus. It is evident that he
travelled every step of the way with Jesus, seeking every op-
portunity to trip him up. Even when Jesus encountered
someone who was possessed, Satan cried out, 'I know who
you are ; you are the Messiah, the Holy One of Israel'.

At first, that seems strange, to have Satan bearing witness
to Jesus, and to who he is. Jesus, however, would not fall into
such a trap. Firstly, he would never accept Satan's assistance
in proclaiming his mission. Satan's motives are always evil. If
the people had heeded the testimony of Satan, they might
have hailed Jesus as the Messiah, and the Holy One of Israel,
without even listening to or heeding the message he proclaimed. At one stage they did actually attempt to hijack his
plans, as they wanted to carry him off to proclaim him king.
If they had succeeded, then Jesus' plan for a kingdom not of
this world, indeed his whole plan of salvation, would have
been twarted.

At a later stage, just as Jesus was headed for Jerusalem, to
complete the task entrusted to him by the Father, Satan made
yet another attempt to stop him. This time it was through
Peter, the leader of the apostles. Out of concern for Jesus' welfare, Peter advised Jesus against going to Jerusalem. On the
surface, it seemed to be sane and common-sense advice.
Jesus, however, was fully alert to the wiles of Satan and,
while his words seemed to be directed at Peter, they were, in
fact, directed at the source of Peter's suggestion: 'Get behind
me, Satan ....'

The work of Jesus was manifold. It was to teach, to preach,
to heal, to drive out demons. This latter part was a very specific area of his ministry. Towards the end of his ministry, as he
was sending his disciples to go forth in his name, he told

them: 'These are the signs that will accompany those who believe: They will drive out demons in my name ... .'

There is a very interesting case in the gospel where the
apostles failed to drive out a demon. A man brought his son
to the apostles and asked them to free him from a demon.
They failed to do so, and when Jesus arrived on the scene, the
man asked him for help and his son was freed. The disciples
asked Jesus why they had failed to drive out the demon, and
he rebuked them for their lack of faith. He had told them that
they were to do this in his name, but they obviously forgot
where the power was, or they failed to fully accept that fact.
St Paul wrote: 'There is no other name given us on earth
whereby we will be saved ... God gave him a name above
every other name, so that at the name of Jesus every knee will
bow, in heaven, on earth, and under the earth, and every
tongue will confess that Jesus Christ is Lord, to the glory of
God the Father.' Satan proclaimed that Jesus was God, but it
certainly wasn't to the glory of God the Father.

Earlier in this chapter, I spoke of Satan being alive and
well, and living on this planet earth. It would be a great mis-
take to imagine that Satan is locked up somewhere called
hell. In the words of Peter, Satan 'wanders around like a roar-
ing lion, seeking whom he may devour'. At the end of time
Satan will certainly be bound, locked up, and be in such a
condition that he will never again be able to oppose God, or
attack any of God's children. There is a story in the gospel
that shows Satan's fear of that final reckoning. A possessed
man lived in a cave, and there were so many demons in him,
that Satan called himself 'legion', because many of his
demons lived within the man. When Jesus was about to drive
them out, Satan begged Jesus not to cast them down into the
abyss. This was a strange request, as if Satan's time for being
cast down had not yet come. It is equally strange that Jesus
granted the request. Jesus ordered the demons to leave the
man, and he permitted them enter a herd of pigs that grazed
close by. The pigs immediately went crazy, ran towards the

cliff and hurled themselves down to their destruction. The very presence of Satan was a presence of death. Later in the gospels we are told that 'Judas took the morsel, and Satan entered into him', and he then went out and hanged himself.

Jesus came 'that we should have life, and have it to the full'. Satan is the harbinger of death, and nothing of what is his can possibly be life-giving. Jesus said the truth would set us free. Satan is the father of lies, and lies are always destructive. Whenever I am authentic I mediate life to others, and when I am not authentic I am mediating death.

Jesus came to redeem the world. The word *redeem* literally means to buy back something or somebody that is sold into bondage or slavery. In earlier ages there were groups of Christians whose apostolate was to redeem captives from slavery, by buying them from their owners and then giving them their freedom. Whenever the gospels speak of Jesus healing people, it also says that 'he drove out demons from those who were afflicted'. His work was one of reclaiming for God that which was God's. 'Render to Caesar the things that are Caeser's, and to God the things that are God's.' He tells the story of a farmer who sowed good wheat in his field. After some time, weeds appeared among the wheat. His workers went to him to report this fact and to ask, 'Was not that good wheat that you sowed? Where did the weeds come from?' The farmer told them that 'an enemy (Satan) has done this.' They asked if they might pull up the weeds, and he told them that he himself would do this, because in attempting to pull up the weeds, they might damage the wheat in the process. Many of us have seen movies portraying false prophets being involved with exorcisms, and the story generally shows the destructive results of such human attempts to do something that only God can do. At the end of his ministry, Jesus announced that Satan's days were numbered, and that 'the prince of this world has already been judged (and condemned, and exposed)'.

'All authority is given to me in heaven and on earth,' Jesus announced. He then went on to make the following extra-ordinary statement: 'I have given you full authority over all the power of the evil one; nothing shall harm you.' When his disciples returned to report on their mission, they announced that 'even the demons obeyed when we spoke in your name'. Jesus brought them one step beyond that when he told them, 'But don't rejoice just because evil spirits obey you; rejoice be-cause your names are registered as citizens of heaven.' Once I enter into kingdom living, I owe nothing anymore to Satan, and he no longer has any claim on me.

Satan is exceedingly cunning, however; hence, Jesus tells us to 'watch and pray, lest you fall into temptation.' He speaks of a demon that was driven out. The demon wandered through lonely places. After some time he returned to the house out of which he had been driven, and found it clean, tidy, and empty, so he went off, got seven more demons. They returned in strength, entered that house, and 'the last state of that house was worse than the first'. Satan is more than will-ing to fill any empty spaces within the human being. That part of us can be filled by God alone, and all attempts to fill it with anything else is fraught with danger. We all know of the dangers of trying to fill that inner emptiness with material goods, with pleasure, or any of the other false gods. In being willing to acknowledge our false gods, we must also be will-ing to name, claim, and tame our own demons.

8 The Shepherd

Love, by definition, is to accept the other where she's at, and to be willing to help her move from there, if and when she wants to move. Incarnation is the story of God coming to us where we're at. God could have loved us from a distance, but he chose not to do things that way. He chose to come among us, to be one of us and one with us, and to move with us to where he would wish to lead us. It never was, and it never is his policy to drive or compel us into anything. This leading is seen in everything he did, including his teaching. He spoke of farmers, of fishermen, of shepherds, of everyday things, to which they could all relate. He began with what they knew, and he brought them from that to something he wanted them to know. Some of his most beautiful and his most simple teachings are based on the role of a shepherd and his sheep, something with which his listeners would have been very familiar.

Let us go back to the Old Testament for a backdrop to all this imagery. God was constantly referring to the people as his sheep, and he himself was going to shepherd them. He condemns their leaders for leaving their people like sheep without a shepherd. The prophet Micah spoke of a vision he had in which 'I saw all Israel scattered on the mountains, like sheep without a shepherd'. I will quote briefly from chapter 34 of Ezekiel, and I would strongly recommend to anyone to read the whole chapter. It summarises the plight of God's people, and his concern for them: 'Prophesy against the shepherds, the leaders of Israel. Give them this message from the sovereign Lord: Destruction is certain for you shepherds who feed yourselves instead of your flocks. Shouldn't shepherds feed their sheep? ... So my sheep have been scattered without a shepherd. ... I myself will search and find my sheep. I will be like a shepherd looking for his scattered flock. I will find my sheep, and rescue them from all the places to which they were scattered ... I will bring them back home ... I myself will tend my sheep ... I will feed them justice.' Jeremiah speaks the following message from God: 'My people have been like lost sheep ... They have lost their way, and cannot remember how to get back to the fold.' This theme is repeated again and again throughout the Old Testament. The Psalmist prays: 'We, your people, the sheep of your flock ... I wander about like a lost sheep.' Because the leaders or the shepherds failed to care for his people, the Lord said that he himself would shepherd them. It was to do that that Jesus came.

To understand Jesus' use of the shepherd theme, it would help enormously to have spent some time in the Holy Land. That of which Jesus spoke is in everyday evidence in that country, right down to the present day. Let me give some simple facts of what I personally witnessed during my few short visits to that country. On the way down to the Dead Sea, passing through what is really a desert, it is remarkable to see the shepherds with their flocks. One wonders what the sheep could possibly be eating as, from the passing coach, all that can be seen is sand and more sand. And yet they obviously can eke out enough wisps of grass to keep them alive. I cannot say what they do for water. What is remarkable is to watch the shepherds. It is a sweltering hot day, it is the noonday sun, and the shepherd is just standing there in the midst of his flock. He has a shepherd's staff, and one or two dogs. He spends his full day like this, with his flock. At night-time, he leads the sheep into a cave in the hillside, and he himself sleeps at the mouth of the cave for the night. A marauder will have to confront the shepherd to get to the sheep. Some of the caves are quite large, and several shepherds with their flocks can share the one cave. The following morning, one of the shepherds leaves the cave, calls out to his sheep, and *his* sheep, and those only, will separate themselves from the larger flock and follow him. A shepherd never drives his flock. He walks on ahead, and his sheep follow him. On several occasions, from the Mount of Thabor, for example, I watched the shepherds in the valley below. The shepherd just walked ahead, and the sheep followed in single file behind. There are frequent thunder storms in the midst of the intense heat. It is said that, in the midst of the most violent storm, the sheep never look up at the sky, but towards the shepherd, as they instinctively gather around him.

It is a common sight to see a shepherd with a sheep or young lamb on his shoulders. The animal has become lame, and is no longer able to keep up with the flock. The shepherd will never abandon one of his sheep. Like a soldier fighting for his country, it is accepted that the shepherd must be willing to die for his sheep. Hence the fact of the shepherd sleeping at the mouth of the cave, or his readiness to repel the attacks of all wild and savage animals. Sometimes a sheep becomes tangled up in briars and has to be freed. Occasionally, a sheep falls down a ravine, and the shepherd will do all within his power to rescue it. It is a very good example of where the rest of the flock are left and the shepherd's full attention is devoted to the one in trouble.

I paint in that background to show what a powerful image Jesus uses when he calls himself the Good Shepherd. This image would be very familiar to his listeners. He uses every dimension of shepherding that was familiar to them. He knows his sheep, and they know him. He is ready to lay down his life for his sheep. If one gets lost, he will leave the ninety-nine and look for the lost one till he has found it. He goes one step further than being a shepherd when he says that he is the very entrance to the sheepfold. To become part of his flock, I have to hear his voice, to answer his call, and allow him lead me into the sheepfold. In another context, Jesus says that 'no one comes to the Father but through me'.

There is no other way of entering the kingdom of God. There is a very important point here. 'I know mine, and mine know me. My sheep know my voice, and they come to me.' To someone like myself, all sheep look alike (except for the few black ones!), but a shepherd would be able to recognise his sheep anywhere, and they would clearly recognise his voice among the greatest babble. It has often amazed me, while driving through the mountains in the west of Ireland and I encounter sheep with their lambs on the road. To me, they are all mixed up, with no obvious groupings within the larger flock. And then a mother bleats a cry, and her lambs run straight to her, and they move off the road together.

Christianity is about knowing Jesus, not just knowing *about* him. He speaks of those who, on the day of judgement, will claim that he walked their roads, and he spoke in their streets, and he will dismiss them with the words, 'Depart from me; I do not know you.' This is the result of their not knowing him, because he stresses that he knows his sheep, and they know him. He makes an interesting comparison between sheep and goats. Among the flocks of sheep there are usually many goats, and they seemingly mingle together with ease. There is one great difference, however, between sheep and goats, besides the obvious ones. The sheep will follow the shepherd anywhere, and at all times. The goats, however, do not have any sense of loyalty. If they are there in the midst of the flock, it is just because they are always ready to follow the crowd. A goat-herd has to drive his goats, because they can never be led. That is what Jesus means when he uses the image of separating the sheep from the goats at the final judgement. The sheep will be those who follow Jesus willingly, and allow themselves to be led by him. The goats, on the other hand, are those who follow Jesus if and when it suits them, but they have no sense of loyalty or obligation in the following. There is an Irish expression which speaks of 'a conversion during a thunder-storm'. The person is terrified, and, in that moment of terror, will promise the Lord anything. This conversion lasts until the thunder-storm passes by!

Jesus speaks of a false prophet in terms of someone who poses as a shepherd, but whose real purpose is to steal the sheep, and to use them for his own benefit. Because of the witness dimension of Christian living, this treachery is all the more reprehensible. It is being a thief in shepherd's clothing. 'All others who came before me were thieves and robbers. ... The thief's purpose is to steal and destroy ... A hired hand will run when he sees a wolf coming. He will leave the sheep because they are not his, and he isn't their shepherd. And so the wolf attacks them, and scatters the flock. The hired hand runs away because he is merely hired, and has no real concern for the sheep.'

Jesus contrasts himself with such false shepherds. He is ready and willing to lay down his life for his sheep. He has come that they may have life, and have it to the full. He speaks of other sheep who are not in his fold at the moment. He announces his intention to seek out those sheep, so that there might be 'one fold and one shepherd'. Sometimes this is interpreted as meaning that there is only one true church, or that there should only be one church. I think this interpretation is wrong. If someone really wants to move to another Christian church, or to become a Christian in any of the churches, well and good. There can be a triumphalism, however, about the merits of one church above the others, and that can show itself in nothing less than what could be called sheep-stealing. I think it is sad if the concentration of one Christian church is in attracting members from another church. There are millions of sheep out there who have no shepherd, who do not belong to any fold, who have no knowledge of, or sense of belonging to God. There are so many sheep out there being ravaged by the wolves in the form of exploiters, expansionists, manipulators, and predators. These are all children of God, who are scattered and defenseless, like sheep without a shepherd. 'It is not the desire

of your heavenly Father that any one of these should be lost.
Pray, therefore, the Lord of the harvests to send shepherds to
lead these people into my fold. I am the gate to that fold, and
there is no other way of entering than through me.'

Jesus said that he was 'sent to the lost sheep of the house
of Israel'. He came to call sinners. The concern of the shepherd for the sheep who is lost is something that was very real
to his listeners. He was condemned because he associated
with sinners, and 'even ate with them'. To that condemnation
he replied that it was for such as these that he had come. His
story of the lost sheep is something that has always and ever
highlighted the core of the Christian message. With a shepherd like Jesus, there is no reason for any of us to be lost.

There are times when we can become entangled in the briars and brambles of life. We cannot pray, we cannot motivate
ourselves, we cannot lift ourselves out of the depression or
the oppression. This can be really difficult to handle. The way
of the spiritually mature is very definite in such circumstances. They 'sit in the pain', as it were, and they wait for
God. In other words, because of their experience of the Good
Shepherd in their lives, they are totally convinced that if they
have the patience to wait and trust, Jesus will come to them,
and set them free. I am not saying they should not pray, no
more than I'm suggesting that the sheep in such circumstances should not, or would not cry out for help. The cry for
help is the prayer for such situations. The important thing,
however, is to believe and trust that such a prayer will be
heard and heeded. It is not possible for a human being to fall
on her knees, cry out to God, and not be heard.

Jesus has many titles in scripture. He is Messiah, the
Christ, the Anointed One, the Holy One of Israel, the Son of
Man, etc. John the Baptist points to Jesus, and announces:
'Behold the Lamb of God, behold him who takes away the sin
of the world.' John's listeners would be quite familiar with
the importance of a lamb being offered in sacrifice for the
forgiveness of sin. This had always been part of the Hebrew

tradition. The lamb is a symbol of innocence. There is nothing so innocent as to see young lambs running and gambolling in a field. The sight is always sure to evoke a thrill of excitement in every child, from one to one hundred. The idea of the innocent paying for the sins of the guilty is something that predated the coming of Jesus, and that found its completion in him. He is the lamb of sacrifice, and 'by his blood we are saved'. We are washed in the blood of the lamb for the forgiveness of sin. Once again, like the teaching about the shepherd and his flock, this would have a more real everyday significance for the people of Jesus' time than it does for us.

One final point about Jesus as shepherd. When we follow him, he then appoints us as shepherds for others, with the instruction to 'feed my lambs; feed my sheep'. It is a beautiful symbol of how Jesus passes responsibility for his mission on to us. When we receive the Spirit, we take over the baton of the relay race, and, in the words of Paul, 'let us run with determination the race that lies before us.' Towards the end of his life Paul says of himself, 'I have done my best in the race; I have run the full distance, I have finished the race. And now the prize awaits me, the crown of righteousness that the Lord, the righteous Judge, will give me on that great day of his return.' When we receive the Power from on high, we becomes witnesses of gospel truths. We accept the responsibility of shepherds with gratitude and humility, because it is pure privilege, and pure choice on the part of God. We confirm the sheep in their worth and sacredness and, in time, we train and entrust them to accept their own vocation of being shepherds for others. The responsibility and the message must be passed on. Each of us is nothing more than a channel, a conduit pipe, an instrument, and we must never fall into the trap of thinking of ourselves as generators, or as the source of any of this glorious and eternal privilege. Many a shepherd has himself/herself become lost in the mist, and some may even have led others into the mist with them.

9 The Friend

A friend is one who is connected to another in intimate confidence, out of goodness, for mutual benefit, and independent of sexual or family love. In today's language we say that a friend is someone who really knows me and still accepts and loves me. In the Old Testament we can easily see a God of fire, brimstone, and commandments. This would be very misleading, as well, of course, as being untrue. In the book of Exodus we read that 'Moses stood before the Lord, who spoke to him as a man speaks to a friend.' The Psalmist speaks quite frequently of God as a friend. 'The Lord is the friend of those who obey him ... Come, my young friends, and listen to me ....' A friend is someone who is on my side, and has my best interests at heart.

Friendship is a special expression of love. There is a sense of continuity about friendship. Some people can make friends, and keep friends, and years and distance never shakes this. This points to something special within, and I believe that something to be of God. When we speak of God's love, we say that God loves us unconditionally. He loves us because he is good, and this is not effected by us being good, bad, or indifferent. The big difference, of course, is that, when we are good, we are open to receiving and experiencing the love of God.

In every sense of the word, and according to every definition, Jesus came to be a friend to all of us sinners. Indeed, he would bring that much further, and refer to us as his brothers and sisters. I cannot exaggerate the importance of allowing Jesus keep both feet on the ground. He came down here to be

with us, and we can easily put him back out of our reach
again. The Word became flesh, and we can run the risk of
turning that flesh back into word again. This all has to do
with religion, with law, with control, whereas Jesus is only interested in surrender, which produces spirituality. To have a
friend, I must be a friend. A friend is someone who travels
the road with us. When Jesus travelled with the two disciples
to Emmaus, although he was a stranger to them at the beginning, they ended up as friends. It is said that a friend is someone I have never met before.

Children have an instinct for friendliness. They make
friends with their pets, and they can talk for hours to imagi-
nary friends. There is a sense of security in having a friend. A
very young child can be very selective about who she goes to,
or who she can trust. The instinct tells the child when a place
is safe. That is why it is such a frightening betrayal of trust
when a child is abducted, molested, or brutalised by someone the child has come to trust. When it comes to the children
of the gospel, I think of Jesus having some sort of magnetic
personality for them. There must have been abundant evidence of all that attracts children, as he spoke, laughed, and re-
laxed. The best image of Jesus here is one of the radiant smile,
the infectious laugh, the open face, and the vibrant personality.
Jesus must have been anything but sullen, dour, solemn, and
all that implies a lack of friendliness. The children were attracted to him, and this was obviously on such a scale as to
annoy the disciples who had more serious business, and
more pressing matters to deal with. The children were getting
in the way, and they had to be got out of the way. Jesus objected
strongly to the stance they took.

A friend always has time, and the other is always made to
feel worthwhile, and important. Jesus put people first at all
times, and this was often at the expense of the law, which was
so important to the religious leaders of his day. If there was a
choice between a human being and a law, the person always
came first. This had to do with lepers, prostitutes, Samaritans,

and tax collectors. His friendship was never exclusive, and it was there, and is there, for anyone who is willing to accept it. I can hold out a hand of friendship forever, but we don't begin to activate that friendship until the other is willing to reach out a hand to me.

One of the greatest characteristics of Jesus was that he was a friend to sinners. This was a real shocker for the religious-minded people of his time. They insisted on expulsions, marginalising, and even stoning to death. The sinner was well outside the boundaries of friendship for such people. Of all the criticisms they made of Jesus, the one they spoke with greatest shock was that he befriended sinners, and even ate with them. That, in their eyes, was an unforgivable sin. By doing that he had put himself outside their very exclusive circle. What made matters worse, from their point of view, is that he defended sinners, and attacked the religious leaders for their attitudes, for their self-righteousness. That was the beginning of the end for Jesus, as far as they were concerned. Jesus was to pay the ultimate penalty for his friendships.

What the religious leaders could not understand, however, and indeed were totally unwilling to understand, was the fact that it was for sinners that Jesus came, and it was for them that he would die. 'Greater love than this no one has, that a person should lay down his life for a friend.' Being with him must have been a most extraordinary experience for the outcasts of his day. It was obvious that he was a very good and holy man, and yet his attitude towards them was to treat them as equals. They never felt that he looked down on them in any way. It would not be possible to have any kind of friendship with another if one considered himself superior to the other. Friendship is based on what we share in common. Because of Incarnation, Jesus shared the human condition with these people, and he 'was like them in all things but sin'.

Jesus attracted people. 'Everybody is looking for you', the apostles told him. Christianity, the message he left to be proclaimed, is all about attraction, and not about promotion.

Wherever he went, huge crowds followed him. They just wanted to be with him, just as one friend enjoys being with the other. If he made any demands on them, it was obviously all for their good, and was spoken out of a genuine love, and not a desire to control.

In the words of scripture, 'He was all things to all men/women.' Even his mother had to wait her turn, because he was busy with those around him. Like any person, Jesus had some special friends for some special occasions. There is always a hierarchy in friendships. No matter how many friends any of us may have, we all have those few very special friends. Jesus would go from the midst of the crowds to being alone with his apostles, and from there he would go aside with Peter, James, and John for those moments of greater intimacy and revelation. They were with him when he was glorified on Thabor, and when he sweated blood in Gethsemane. John has no hesitation whatever in calling himself 'the disciple whom Jesus loved'. At the Last Supper, we are told that John leaned on Jesus' breast as Jesus spoke. In today's world, all of that could very well be whispered about, but such open intimacies between friends, be they male or female, were very acceptable in the culture of those times.

Jesus had other special friends outside of the immediate circle of apostles. Lazarus, and his two sisters, Martha and Mary, were special friends. It is implied in the gospels that he would go to them from time to time, just to get away from it all. Bethany is but a short distance outside Jerusalem, and, by going out there, he could be 'far from the madding crowd' for a day or two. The gospel tells us that Jesus loved Lazarus and his sisters. When Lazarus was sick, Jesus was told, 'The one whom you love is ill.' Jesus spoke of Lazarus as his friend. When Jesus came to Bethany, Martha ran to meet him. Jesus was by far the most important person to call on her in her time of mourning. When Mary met Jesus, she said 'Lord, if you had been here my brother would not have died.' Mary trusted Jesus' love sufficiently to believe that, somehow,

Jesus would never have allowed Lazarus to die. When Jesus came to the tomb of Lazarus, he wept openly and unashamedly. The onlookers remarked, 'See how much he loved him'. Lazarus and his sisters were obviouly good people, and, in the words of the Psalmist, 'The Lord is the friend of those who obey him.' Later, Jesus would tell his apostles, 'If you love me, you will obey me.'

It is fascinating to see Jesus befriending and defending the most marginalised in the society of his day. Speaking to the Samaritan woman at the well was something that was totally unacceptable to the Jewish mentality. Not only did he speak to her, but he took time out to be with her, and to be there for her. What he did, what he said, and the person that he was, touched her so deeply that she ran off and brought her friends to meet Jesus.

The woman taken in adultery, who was being stoned to death, was bottom of the pile as far as the religious leaders were concerned, and yet he defended and befriended her. He spoke to her with respect, and he remained with her when all the others had walked away. The stance he took on her behalf was heroic, and, indeed, reckless. Jesus was never a fair-weather friend. He is still there for all of us, when everyone else and everything else has let us down. He is 'the same yesterday, today, and always.' 'He is always faithful …', Paul reminds us, and fidelity is one of the cornerstones of friend-ship.

The role of friendship requires versatility. Sometimes a friend has to be bailed out of a situation and, when we are facing difficult situations, it is vital to have a friend around for a helping hand, a listening ear, or a comforting shoulder.

One look at the widow of Naim, as she accompanied the dead body of her only son, and Jesus was fully available to her in her hour of darkness. A man was lowered through the roof on a stretcher by his friends, and Jesus was immediately ready to respond to both their faith and their love. His friends were being tossed around on the stormy sea, and they feared for their lives but Jesus, once again, was there as their friend. A friend is faithful, dependable, and reliable. It is when we are in trouble that we find out who our real friends are. Again and again we read that Jesus had pity on the crowds who were hungry, tired, or without any sense of belonging. He often brought his disciples aside 'to rest for a while', because he saw that they were tired. Sensitivity is part of friendship. On many occasions he had reason to correct his disciples when they failed to understand the simple basics of friendship. They were arguing among themselves about who was the greatest, something that should have no part in friendship. Even when Judas used his friendship with Jesus as a means of betraying him, Jesus still called him friend.

The Last Supper, and the discourse of Jesus at that time, is a beautiful expression of his friendship. He goes on his knees and, in humble service, he washes their feet. He says that, because he told them all about himself, they must no longer consider themselves as slaves or servants, because a master never treats his servants with such intimacy. 'You are my friends ...', he told them. He laid great stress on the fact that they were to remain very close to him if they wanted to survive. His friendship would give them life, just as the branch draws its life from the vine. He is going to give them everything that is his, and they are going to share as full partners in his kingdom. By promising them the Spirit, he is enrolling them for eternity in the life of the Trinity, and he promies that 'We will come and make our abode in you ...' He is not going to desert them or abandon them in the storm. He will be with them always, even to the end of time. And, he adds, even if heaven and earth were to pass away, his word or promise to them will never pass away. This is very powerful friendship language. He prays for them to his Father, and he asks the Father to 'keep them safe whom you have given to me'. He is going to prepare a place for them, so that one day he will return to bring them with him in an eternal friendship of love, presence and completeness.

Yes indeed, a friend is someone who travels with us. Jesus travels with us to the very end, and then the full joy of the friendship will be realised. He offers us his joy, his peace, and his abundant life. None of us could ever claim an earthly human friendship like that. However, because Jesus came 'to do and to teach', he teaches us, and clearly demonstrates what real friendship is, before he asks us to 'do the same for each other'. 'I have given you an example to follow. Do as I have done to you. You know these things, now do them.' Only God is constant. Friendships that last, and that are life-living, are the outcome of the presence of God's Spirit. God is love, and all expressions of real love are offshoots of God's love.

When Jesus asks us to love others as he loves us, he knows only too well that, of ourselves, such a task is impossible for us. That is why he promises to send the Holy Spirit. 'Then', he said, 'you will be my witnesses to the ends of the earth.' Christian living has a witness value at its core. It is significant that when Christians first appeared on the scene, and nobody seemed to know or understand who or what they were, the observers came to an unanimous verdict when they remarked, 'See how these Christians love one another'.

10 The Leader

The whole saga of salvation revolves around the fact of a people who had gone astray, who were lost, and who could not find their way back home. From the time of the Fall there was a sense of exile among the human race. They were restless on the face of the earth, as if they were a people in exile from the garden. They built themselves a very high tower that would reach to the sky. 'This will bring us together, and keep us from scattering all over the world.' But God was having none of it! No matter how they themselves tried to 'fix' things, they were in exile from their true home, and there is no way they could ever get back there on their own, or through their own devices. Throughout the Old Testament, the prophets were God's leaders, sent to give his people a sense of direction towards the good, and towards the truth. The actual historical/ geographical exiles in Egypt and in Babylon were symbolic of the real exile from the garden. The Old Testament is replete with references to God's promise to 'bring the exiles home'.

Having a base, a homeland, was vitally important to the Hebrews, just as it is to the Jews in Israel today. To this very day they continue to return from exile. Their earthly dream of a land 'flowing with milk and honey' was a very real image of their true home. They were not at home anywhere else on this earth. In the very last book of the Bible, the Book of Revelations, John calls heaven 'the New Jerusalem'. It is there, and only there, that God's people will ever feel at home. The most significant exile of the Hebrews was in Egypt. They were in slavery, with no hope of freedom.

God chose Moses, and commissioned him to lead his people out of bondage. At first, Moses was reluctant to accept such a responsibility, but God insisted that he do so. The Lord would be his strength and his protection. What followed was an extraordinary revelation and display of the Lord's power. Although it was Moses who was leading them, it was obvious that the Lord himself was opening up the way for them. He provided shade against the scorching sun by day, and heat against the freezing desert by night. He let fall their daily supply of bread (manna) from heaven, and from the rock flowed abundant water to quench their thirst. For forty years, they made their weary way back from exile, back to a land chosen for them by God, which they called the Promised Land. Their sojourn in the desert was a continuous unfolding of the Lord's care for them, and his personal involvement in their delivery from bondage.

This journey from Egypt is a very real, and a very powerful foreshadowing of the journey to salvation unfolded by Jesus. The Lord himself has come to lead us from slavery and bondage into the freedom of the children of God. Jesus would be our Moses, leading us through the desert of life into the kingdom of God. Not only would he lead us, but he himself would be the manna for the journey. This is more than just eucharist. It is the 'daily bread' he told us to ask for. In the days of the manna, it was meant for the present day only. It was an act of trust in God to accept that he would provide the manna for the following day. On one occasion, with their lack of trust, the people gathered manna to store it for the following day, and they found that it wasn't edible. Jesus offered himself as the rock from which flowed the water, when he cried out, 'If anyone is thirsty, let that person come to me ... The water I will give takes away thirst altogether. It becomes a perpetual spring within them, giving them eternal life.'

A leader is someone who goes ahead, who faces the dangers first. He himself would take on the sin, the sickness, and the death. In doing this he would open up the Red Sea, so that we might cross over in safety to the Promised Land. He never asks us to do something he himself has not done. From the very moment of his commissioning in the Jordan waters, he faced Satan alone in the desert. At the end of his life, in the garden of Gethsemane, he told the soldiers who had come to arrest him, 'I am the one you came to arrest, so let the others go.' He was always prepared to stand between his disciples and danger. He promised that, even after he left them to return to his Father, he would never abandon them in the storm. The purpose of sending the Spirit was to lead them into all truth, and in that truth they would be free. At every step of the way, Jesus was very conscious that these people would never make it alone. They were 'like sheep without a shepherd'; they had no one to lead them. That is why they followed him with such enthusiasm. At long last they had found someone who knew where he was going. This is very important in a leader. His very presence breathes confidence in those around. When Jesus was arrested, and the apostles experienced vulnerability and isolation, they were terrifed and they scattered in all directions.

Jesus had very harsh words for the Jewish leaders. They were wolves in sheep's clothing, and they did not have the welfare of his followers at heart. He told them that they should call no one on earth their leader. He, and he alone, was the one who came to deliver them. His form of leadership was so totally different from that to which the people were familiar. When he washed the apostles' feet, he told them that his leadership was one of service. The greatest one among them is the one who serves. This service is leadership at its best. In his kingdom, the lowly are raised up, and the mighty are brought down. Anyone who believes himself to be first is, in fact, last in the priority of his kingdom. This is not leading from behind, but travelling alongside. The leadership was one of accompaniment. It is to be an equal among equals.

Such teaching must have sent shock-waves among the religious leaders who listened to him. This man was out to destroy them, and so they decided that he should be removed before he went on to do more damage, and to deprive them of something they saw as their divine right. Their complete authority was something that ran totally contrary to everything for which Jesus stood.

Jesus appeared to his apostles many times after his resurrection. It was very important that they be left in no doubt that he was alive and well. He had passed safely through the portals of death, and he returned to confirm that fact. He was the one who had opened up the Red Sea for them. At the moment of his death, the veil in the temple was torn in two. He had opened the way for them into the Holy of Holies, where God dwells. They could follow him through life, and through death. He would go ahead to prepare a place for them. He would then return to bring them, so that where he was, they also would be. He would be with them right out to the very end, and beyond. His was a very definite and confident leadership, that inspired confidence and loyalty in those who followed him. Unlike Moses, Jesus would accompany his followers into the Promised Land, and he would be there to share his eternal victory with them.

Consistency is one of the qualities of good leadership. People should not be led one direction today, and another tomorrow, depending on the latest fad. From the very outset of his mission, Jesus had a very clear mandate, a very clear message, and nothing could deflect him from that. The religious leaders deliberately misunderstood or twisted what he had to say. Jesus came back at them on all occasions. Some of his listeners walked away, because they could not accept what he was saying. He didn't run after them, or make any attempt to alter the content of his message. He announced that they were either with him or against him; they were free to follow him or not. His mention of being a king was misinterpreted, and they wanted to take him off and crown him as their king. Jesus would never ever countenance such distractions from the direction in which he had directed his life, and in which he intended to lead his followers.

Jesus was always on the move, and he refused to remain on in places where his on-going presence was requested. 'There are other cities to which I must go', he announced. Even while he stood in the midst of the people, they had a sense of being led. His very words gave direction to their lives. The throngs followed him from one part of the country to the other. At times, this brought them far from home, and into wild and barren places. When they had nothing to eat there, he fed them, rather than have them unable to follow him, or return home because of weakness and hunger.

The very energy God gives me with which to follow him is the very same energy I can use if I wish to walk away. In following him, however, I can avail of a Higher Power that is always at my disposal. With the call to follow comes the grace to respond to the call. God won't send me anywhere when I die; rather will he eternalise the direction of my life right now. Following him leads to life. The rich young man refused to leave all things to follow him. This saddened Jesus, because the young man was so blinded by his earthly wealth and attachments that he totally failed to see the eternal riches to which Jesus invited him. Jesus would never force him, or anyone else, to follow him. A basic human right, given us by God himself, is that of free will, and God would never ever encroach on that. The invitation to follow comes from him; the decision to follow must come from us.

After Jesus had left them and the Spirit had come, Peter and the other apostles were arrested and brought before the council. They were reminded that they had been told never again to preach in the name of Jesus, and they had continued to do so. Peter spoke to them about Jesus, about him being sent by God, and about how they had killed the Holy One of God. He then went on to tell them that Jesus was raised from the dead, and that God has brought him to his right hand 'as Leader and Saviour'.

The centrality of Jesus' role in leading us back to the Father is something that continues for all time. His words, his

Spirit, and his presence leads us still. 'We have decided to follow Jesus' is the title of a Christian song. In the early church, the disciples were called 'Followers of the Way', clearly showing that being part of the community was the result of deciding to be led by Jesus, and by his message. Today, in movies about life from other planets, in space movies about aliens coming among us, we are familiar with the phrase 'Bring me to your leader'. In other words, I want to know from whence you come, and where is the source of your being. The life of the Christian must always give witness to the reality of Jesus, and to the totally involved nature of his presence among us.

In his own life, we read of Jesus 'being led by the Spirit into the desert ... into the Temple'. A life without inspiration is purposeless and aimless. We all need direction in life. We seek spiritual direction, we look for direction and purpose, we set goals and aims. There is a basic insecurity that is part of human living. From the time of the Fall there is a nomadic quality to our existence. 'We have not here a lasting city,' Paul tells us, 'but we look for one that is to come, which will be revealed in Christ Jesus.' Without Jesus we are completely adrift on the sea of life. The apostles waited for Jesus, but when he didn't come, they set out across the Sea of Galilee without him. Needless to say they soon found themselves in the midst of a treacherous storm. They would have drowned had not Jesus come to them on the waters, to take control of the situation. 'And when Jesus got into the boat, immediately they were where they were going.'

In Jesus we have a leader, as well as a plan and purpose for life. Being led by him is an end in itself, in so far as heaven begins now, and the kingdom of God is among us. As we travel with him, then, like Paul, we can look forward to completing the journey, and to begin our eternal prayer: 'Free! Free at last! I thank my God we are free at last!'

11 The Son

It often helps in our understanding of a word if we know where the word came from and what is its meaning at origin. Take, for example, the word *family. Familia* is the Latin for household, and *famulus* is the Latin for servant. Therefore, we can assume that the root meaning of the word has to do with belonging, and with service. Accepting the privilege of belonging must also include the responsibility of service within the household. While not daring to attempt an understanding of what is mystery, we can know much of what is deity. All three Persons of the Trinity are equally involved in such revelation. Jesus came to become one of us, so we might become part of what is divine. He uses language that is familiar to us, as we relate to each other. Grace builds on nature, rather than replacing it. Jesus spoke familiar words like father, son, brother, sister, and family. Before he was ready to show us who we are, and who we can become, he went to great length to show us who he is.

Jesus called himself Son of God, and he spoke of God as his Father. To fully understand this language, it would help if we thought of those words with the mind-set of his listeners. The bond between father and son was inalienable in the time of Jesus. Everything of what was life passed from father to son. What the father owned belonged to the son also, by nature of the relationship. 'All I have is yours', the father told the brother of the Prodigal Son. The whole point of the story is to show the need of the father to restore his wayward son to equal right within the family, no matter how much he had attempted to live outside of that unit. The family was a sacred

entity, and it was the responsibility of every father to preserve that entity. It is not possible for our modern western
minds to fully grasp the extraordinary implications of Jesus'
claim on God as his Father, and to proclaim himself Son of
God. This was language that was totally blasphemous to the
ears of the leaders, because of their understanding of God.
God was in the burning bush, the fire and brimstone, and the
plagues of Egypt. The chasm between the human and divine
was infinite, and it was not within their competence to visualise a coming together of those extremes. Through incarnation, God became one with us, right down to the words and
language we use to speak of God. If God is infinite in everything, then he is infinitely simple. The most profound truths
are capable of being expressed in the simplest language. If
God wanted to give us a sense of belonging, he could choose
no simpler or, indeed, more profound way than to bring us
into a relationship with him that is one of family. Jesus called
God Father, and he taught us to pray to God by calling him
'Our Father …'

As I've said already, the relationship between son and father
was an unique one with the Hebrew culture. The greatest
treachery they could envisage was that inflicted by a son
against his father. Abraham was tested to the very limits
when he was asked to sacrifice his son, Isaac. I believe that
Abraham had to live with the reality of this for a while, with
all its horrible implications, even if we in hindsight could not
imagine a God who would demand such abject subservience.
God, as we know, did not go through with this demand, but
Abraham's willingness to comply is given us as the supreme
act of obedience. In Jesus, God himself would go through
with his promise and sacrifice his own Son and, for those
who accept the full ramifications of this, he would be seen to
have given us the highest possible expression of his love for
us.

Jesus, while being Son of God was, of course, God himself.
Therefore, because of his union with the Father, his will was

totally in tune with the will of the Father. 'I never say any-thing unless the Father tells me. I and the Father are one. They who see me, see the Father.' This was at the core of Jesus' message. It would be totally and completely to miss the whole thrust of the gospels to think of Jesus as one ex-pression of the deity, and to retain the possibility of there being another expression with a different agenda.

Many of us grew up with the concept of God as some old man, with a long white beard, away up in the sky some-where, who continually kept tabs on us, and who was always ready to confront us with our wrong-doings. There is only one God, and that is the God of the gospels, the God who is revealed in the person and in the message of Jesus. At the Last Supper, Philip asked Jesus, 'Lord, show us the Father, and we will be satisfied.' Jesus replied, 'Philip, don't you even yet know who I am, even after all the time I have been with you? Anyone who has seen me has seen the Father. So why are you asking to see him? Don't you believe that I am in the Father, and the Father is in me? The words I say are not my own, but my Father who lives in me does his work through me. Just believe that I am in the Father, and the Father is in me. Or at least believe because of what you have seen me do.'

I have quoted this at some length, because of all the chap-ters in this book, this is one in which I could do nothing better than let Jesus speak for himself! His relationship with his Father was a constant theme, and it is my belief that if I could believe and accept this truth, I would actually be in total ac-ceptance of the core of the gospel message.

Original sin was one of disobedience. The fall of Lucifer was the result of refusing to serve. In himself, Jesus came to turn all of that around irrevocably. His whole life would be one of total obedience to the Father, and his death would be the greatest expression of that obedience. 'My very meat is to do the will of him who sent me.' Jesus spent many hours, late at night, in prayer to the Father. It was after such times that he

chose his apostles, that he presented his core teachings on the
Mount, that he faced his trial and his death. It was as if he
were continually checking in with his Father for the latest instructions. I am not saying that Jesus himself didn't know
what to do. What I mean is that, by listening to the Father, he
was doing the Father's will and not his own. In Gethsemane
he prayed, 'Father, if it is possible let this chalice pass from
me; but not my will but yours be done.' Jesus had, of course, a
will and a mind of his own. He had to have this to be able to
claim his own personhood. He was not a programmed robot,
nor was he the victim of some unalterable predestination. Of
his own free will and choice he chose to do the Father's will
in everything, because the evil he came to redress was the
outcome of disobedience and of self-will run riot.

God is love, and all revelations about the Father is of one
who loves without condition. The story of the Forgiving
Father, which is usually called the Prodigal Son, is a resumé
of the kind of love in question. The Father waits and longs for
the son's return. There are no remonstrations, no condemna-
tions, and no conditions attaching to the son's return to the
family. The father even supplies sandals for the son, something that was worn only when travelling. In other words,
the son was free to leave again if he wanted to. The father's
love was total and unconditional. 'I know the Father. No one
knows the Father except the Son, and those to whom the Son
chooses to reveal him.' Because Jesus knew the Father, he
painted a picture to show something of what his Father was,
and of how he deals with his children. This Father loves because he is good, and nothing changes that, whether a child is
good, bad, or indifferent.

In a way, the Father is like a large umbrella that Jesus
opens out, and invites us to gather underneath. We are invited
to stand under the Niagara of his love. In the Old Testament,
God offered himself as the only God, and the people were invited to become his people. This was a God-subject relationship, where the emphasis was laid on the responsibilities of

the subject. They were to adore, to serve, and to fear their God. The relationship was based on commandment and edict, and the rewards were acquired, earned, and merited. Jesus changed all of that irrevocably. He offered a God who was Father, and the people were invited to become his children. In fact, Jesus went so far as to state that, unless they became like children, they could not enter the home of his Father. God has no grandchildren. We are all his children, in close and direct relationship. This relationship was based on love, rather than law, and the commandments were replaced with the responsibility of loving God, and loving neighbour.

In fact, Jesus went so far as to put these two on an equal footing, and he declared that whatever we do for others is accepted by him as being done for him. If God is our Father, then we become brothers and sisters. He said that he and the Father are one; and he now adds that he and each of us are called to be one. 'Father, I pray that they may be one, just as you and I are one; that just as you are in me, and I am in you, so they will be in us, and the world will believe that you sent me.' It is extraordinary, if not frightening, to think that Jesus hinged the whole credibility of his message on the evidence of our love for each other. 'Where there is love, there is God. They who live in love, live in God, and God lives in them.' The religious leaders of his day based their whole teaching on a love of law. There is no way they could understand, or were prepared to accept a law of love.

Of all the things Jesus said, nothing upset them more than that he called himself God's Son. This was blasphemy and, therefore, merited death. Yes, indeed, Jesus called himself the Son of God, and his doing so would lead very predictably to his death. It is ironic that what the leaders saw as rightful and deserved punishment, was seen by God as the logical expression of unbounded love. 'Greater love than this no one has, than to lay down a life for a friend.'

In the previous chapter I spoke of Jesus as our Moses, bringing us into the Promised Land. As the Son of God, he leads us right into the family of God. 'Who are my mother, and my brothers, and my sisters? Those who do the will of my Father in heaven are my mother, my brothers, and my sisters.' Belonging to the family qualifies us to receive the full benefit of family inheritance, and of privilege. He tells us that we can ask the Father for anything in his name, and we will receive it. Our membership in God's family entitles us to full access to the treasuries of heaven. 'The Father will surely give the Spirit to those who ask him.' In this is salvation completed, when the Father, Son, and Spirit come to live in us. ' ... and We will make our home in him.' Redemption is now complete.

In his prayer to the Father at the Last Supper, Jesus prays, 'And now I am coming to you ... I have given them your word ... And I give myself entirely to you, so that they might be entirely yours.' With his dying breath, Jesus submitted himself to his Father: 'I have finished the work that you gave me to do ... Into your hands I commend my spirit.' He promised that he would send his Spirit to complete his work in us. The Spirit would remind us of all he had told us. 'This is not a Spirit of fear', Paul tells us, 'but a Spirit of sonship that would enable us to cry out Abba, Father.'

12 The Servant

Through the prophet Isaiah, God spoke of the Messiah he would send, with these words: 'Look at my Servant, whom I have chosen ...' In his teaching, Jesus said that the greatest in his kingdom are those who serve. Because he had come to 'do and to teach', in that order, it is essential that his life is seen as one of service first, and teaching second. His whole life was one of obedience to the Father through his service of his people. In Jesus' day, there were two groups of Levites who served in the Temple. There was one group who served God directly through the offering of sacrifices, and the second group who served the people who came to the Temple. Jesus connected both levels of service by equating them in importance. 'The first commandment is loving God ... and the second is like this, loving one's neighbour.' Jesus would go further in the connection between both when he said that what we did for others, he would take as being done for himself.

When he washed the feet of his apostles, Jesus gave them a powerful example of service. He took off his cloak, wrapped a towel around his waist, and poured water into a basin. This must have brought gasps of astonishment from the apostles, because this was exactly the way in which a slave performed his tasks. This was a much more powerful image of service than it might appear to our western eyes today. No wonder Peter was so shocked as to object, and to refuse to let Jesus stoop so low as to minister to him. Jesus insisted, however, and to Peter's further objections, he said, 'Unless you let me wash your feet, you cannot be one of my disciples.' This probably shocked Peter some more, but, with his usual effusiveness, he told Jesus to wash not just his feet, but his head and hands as well. If being willing to accept such lowly service from Jesus was a condition for living in his kingdom, then Peter would accept it. Peter had not understood Jesus' earlier words about the greatest in his kingdom being the one who serves.

Away back at the time of the presentation of Jesus in the Temple, Simeon had prophesied 'This child shall be a sign of contradiction ...' In such humble service, he certainly was a total contradiction to the accepted norms of his day. His kingdom was not of this world, and its teachings were diametrically opposed to the values and norms of the world. In his kingdom, the last shall be first, the first shall be last. The greatest people are those who serve; it is in giving that we receive, and it is in dying that we enter into life. This was revolutionary in the extreme, something I would like to explore in the following chapter.

Jesus was always prepared to walk that extra mile with another. He offered to accompany the centurion to where his servant was. This would also have been prompted by his admiration for one in such a position of authority having such concern for a slave. He travelled with Jairus to his home, and he went out to Bethany to be with Martha and Mary in their hour of bereavement. His whole disposition was one of giving. This, of course, would be brought to the extreme on Calvary, when he gave till it was all gone. He had spoken about this level of giving on many occasions. 'The person who seeks to save his life will lose it ...' What we keep for ourselves will die when we die. Only that which we have given to others will take on an eternal value. In fact, he made this the criterion for general judgement. Not even a cup of cold water, given in his name, will go unrewarded. The theme of his judgement will be scandalously materialistic. He will not ask about religious experience, or religious observance. He will ask about food, clothes, water, and about the kindly concern for others. This must have been a complete turn-up for the books! No wonder the religious leaders were outraged. This man was a very dangerous revolutionary, and must be got rid of, before he destroys the whole fabric of their cherished way of being and of living.

The Magnificat is a wonderful hymn of praise and exultation. It also provides some very helpful insights into God. He is a God who fills the hungry, who cherishes the poor, and who dismisses from his company those who refuse to share with others from their surfeit. He raises up the down-trodden, and he knocks the mighty from their high perches. On the surface, this may seem harsh and unjust. Certainly, from a merely human perspective, it is difficult to promote or to defend. No wonder Paul prays that we might have 'that mind that was always in Christ Jesus'. Without the Spirit of God in our hearts, we could never hope to see anything with the mind and heart of Christ. It is the work of the Spirit to teach us, and to bring us into an awareness and an acceptance of truth, as Jesus proposes it.

The whole attitude of the Christian is best summarised in Jesus' teaching which we call the beatitudes. This is a way of being. It summarises the main qualities of Christian behaviour which, of course, run totally contrary to worldly wisdom and expectations. The really rich people are those who are detached from earthly wealth. Jesus never confused riches with material possessions. He declares those rich who are free from the bondage of earthly wealth. He proclaims those powerful who turn the other cheek and forgive. The greatest are the gentle and the meek; and the true heroes in his kingdom are those whose life-style draws the wrath and opposition of the world. In all of this is something that, in our better moments, we must see as being highly attractive, if not daunting. 'Freedom's just another word for nothing left to lose.' This teaching is scary, because it touches the raw nerve of our insecurities. This is, indeed, a very clear example of our need for the enlightenment of the Spirit of truth, because these are gospel truths that, of ourselves, as human beings, we never could grasp or embrace. Such concepts are outside the boundaries of the natural, materialistic, human mind. 'They also serve who only stand and wait' is one of the many paradoxes of service. It is not about achieving anything. It is a way of being. There is power and strength in meekness and gentleness. Such people 'possess the land', Jesus says. The one who is pure of heart, who is not embroiled in hidden and selfish agendas, is the one who sees God.

Religion, divorced from service of others, is a travesty of everything that God is, or wants. The story of the Good Samaritan is a case in point. The religious people refused to help, because they had some religious commitment or obligation which needed their attention. The Samaritan, on the other hand, was seen by them as someone who had 'no religion.' He did not belong to the lofty heights of the high and mighty. Perhaps the significance in this is, from his lower perspective, he was much more aware of what was going on around him. This is the whole point of Incarnation, when Jesus surrendered his place in the highest heavens, and came down to the level of the lowliest sinner. 'Though he was in the form of God, Jesus did not count equality with God a thing to be grasped. He emptied himself, taking the form of a servant, and became as human beings are.' Note 'as human beings *are*', not just as human beings *look*. This perspective is a very important dimension of service. Jesus went further still when he went on his knees, at ground level, with a basin of water. The ministry of the Samaritan was given without expectation of anything in return. It is covenant, rather than contract. A contract with another implies equal responsibility to meets each other's expectation in the action. I give the shopkeeper some money, and I expect to receive the item I have come to purchase. I can easily break a contract, by cancelling an order, or failing to pay my debts. A covenant, on the other hand, is a contract under seal, to which I can be unfaithful, but which cannot be broken. It implies loyalty, fidelity, and a sense of something that survives. It includes services freely given, without the condition of remuneration. Jesus is involved in humble service, and he allows the receiver the freedom of the response. The nine lepers who were healed did not have their leprosy return just because they failed to give thanks!

The ministry which Jesus entrusted to his apostles was one of service. Freely they had received, so freely they were to give. They were not to work for earthly reward, because their reward would be in heaven. Through this kind of ministry, they could lay up treasures in heaven, where neither the moth nor the rust could destroy. The harvest is great, and they are to pray the Lord of the harvest to send more servants into his harvest. They were to be vigilant in their work, and happy are those whom the Lord finds alert when he returns. In Jesus' own words, 'I will gird myself and minister to them.' This is remarkable. Even at his final coming, instead of judging those who are alert, he is prepared to minister to them. The greatest thanks I can give Jesus for dying for me, is to willingly accept all that he earned for me. Like Peter, we should come to the point of being willing to allow him wash 'my head and my hands as well'.

In the catechism of some years back, we were told that 'God created us to know, love, and serve him ...' Jesus tells us that when we serve, we are still, and always will be, unprofitable servants, in that we are doing the very thing we were created to do. If we are to be disciples of the Servant Lord, then service for others should be our trademark.

Love, by its nature, has to continually express itself. In other words, love must always be a witness. The witness of the early Christians was so evident that the pagans remarked 'See how these Christians love one another'. The Acts of the Apostles gives many details of the ways in which this love was expressed, through the various ways of sharing and of ministering to one another. They were known as Followers of the Way, and they continued to live as Jesus lived, and as he taught them to live. Jesus had come to serve, not to condemn. He really had nothing of earthly value to share with others, but he certainly shared all he did have with them. He gave them his time, he gave them his interest, he gave them, above all, his love. On occasions, he spent so much time with the crowds that his apostles were exhausted. He sent them off to rest, while he himself continued to care for the people and to send them on their way home. This, on many occasions, left himself so exhausted that he slept soundly in the boat at the height of a violent storm. In his service he gave of himself, and in his death he would give himself totally, and there is no greater love than that.

God is love. Jesus was the Father's most real, evident, and down-to-earth expression of his love. Jesus was God's love incarnate, God's love in a body. In Jesus, the Father's love had hands, feet, and a voice. Paul gives a wonderful definition of love: 'Love is patient and kind. Love is not jealous, or boastful, or proud, or rude. It is never glad about injustice, but rejoices whenever the truth wins out. Loves never gives up, is always hopeful, and endures through every circumstance.' Paul has much more to say about love. To all of that we could add, 'Love is caring, always watchful for the welfare of the other, and always puts others first. It is humble in its service, and enriching in its giving. It is devoted, it is constant, and it is entirely reliable at all times.' In the early Christian church, when the historical memory of the man Jesus was still fresh in the mind, Jesus is often referred to as the Servant of God. 'The God of our ancestors has given divine glory to his Servant Jesus ... And so God chose his Servant, and sent him at first to you ... the signs that were preformed in the name of his Servant Jesus ... God, you will not allow your faithful Servant to rot in the grave.'

In his preview of the judgement, Jesus tells us that he will welcome his followers into his kingdom with these words: 'Well done, good and faithful servants. Enter into the joy of the Lord.' It is of the nature of Christian service to be faithful to the end, just as Jesus taught us, through his words and, especially through the shining example of his life and death.

13 The Rebel

Some years ago, at the height of the Chairman Mao reign in China, revolutions were the order of the day. Some high-minded idealists and subversives began to speak a common language; many of the intelligensia, especially the younger and more disillusioned, were pouring forth revolutionary rhetoric, and modern guerrilla warfare came into existence. It was as if a generation had come on board who were fed up with the feudal serfdom of all that went before. There was need for a change to meet the new thinking of a new age. Consolidated authoritarianism, high-security investment, and plain simple greed, do not like the idea of change. Change means letting go, and venturing into something that may not be totally controllable or predictable. This scares them, because of all that they stand to lose in the process. The powers-that-be have always resisted every attempt to change a system over which they had control, and which was built on their best interests. Revolutionaries were seen as danger-ous, unscrupulous, and certainly not mentally stable. They were seen as destructive by nature, and not as people who set out to build, to reform, to improve what went before. Such people stirred up every ounce of paranoia in the minds and hearts of those under threat, and their elimination from the formula, by whatever means, was the only way of preserving the *status quo*. Many of these so-called revolutionaries were noble and idealistic souls, inspired by a thirst for justice, and by a righteous indignation at the injustices they witnessed on a daily basis. Mahatma Ghandi and Martin Luther King come to mind as people who hoped to change the way things were,

and to do so without destructive violence, or without replacing one form of tyranny with another. There have been revolutions that toppled the oppressors, to be replaced by those
who became even more authoritarian and oppressive than
those they removed. This usually resulted when the revolutionaries were clear on what was to be eliminated, but totally
ignorant about what should replace it. It is easy, then, for
their own egos and ambitions to become ends in themselves.

I believe Jesus to be the greatest revolutionary, the greatest
rebel the world has ever seen. A rebel is someone who refuses
to conform to the way things are. He refuses to be bound into
a system he sees as unjust and unacceptable. Jesus came with
no less a mandate than to change the world, and the history
of the world for all time. The overall purpose for Incarnation,
for Jesus coming among us, was to reverse the results of the
Fall, to redeem the children of God who were caught up in a
mesh of deceit and untruths. When Adam and Eve fell for the lie
in the garden, the human race came under new management,
came under the influence of Satan, the father of lies.

There was one particular dimension of our human condition that required the personal intervention of Jesus. This had
to do with the aberrations that had crept into how the religious leaders of the day saw themselves before God. To accept what they stood for, to listen to what they taught, and to
see all this as being right and just, and in accordance with
God's will and plan, that was something that was really offensive in God's eyes. When we see the righteous indignation
of Jesus as he cleared the Temple with a whip of cords, we get
some idea of how he saw things as they were. His upending
of the tables, his scattering of the money, his routing of the
sellers, is highly significant of the zeal and the attitude he
brought to the task of restoring the proper balance between
God and his creatures. He pointed to this again when he
spoke of rendering to Caesar what is Caesar's, and to God
what is God's.

The Pharisees and the religious leaders had the whole system tied up and under their control. The people were hide-bound by laws, rules, and regulations. The role of the scribes was full-time interpretation of the law, while the Pharisees were full-time enforcers of the law. All righteousness was invested in the strict observance of the law.

Imagine the shock waves when Jesus announced that he was replacing this love of law with his law of love! Imagine the gasps of horror, and the rumblings of outrage when he suggested that their Temple would be destroyed, and that it really didn't matter where people worshipped their God, as long as this was done in spirit and in truth. They prided themselves on being children of Abraham, and they reminded Jesus of this fact. This was their way of declaring their heritage and the legitimacy of their religion. Jesus retorted that God could raise up children of Abraham from the very stones that lay on the ground around them.

Jesus reminded them of the many exceptions that were allowed in situations past when, for example, the people were hungry and they were permitted eat the bread that had been made sacred by being offered in the Temple. He showed them how they had squeezed all the elements of humanity out of the law and had come up with something that was controlling, unfeeling, and completely insensitive to the reality of human living. Their law was a body without a soul, and it could never be life-giving. Because he had come that they should have life he, therefore, had to confront the religious leaders on all and every aspect of the law, and their application of it.

There was a prophetic dimension to his teaching. A prophet is not someone who foretells the future, but someone who interprets the present, speaks God's word in the present, and condemns what is wrong and evil in that present. No wonder prophets often ended up as martyrs, because it often happens that the messenger gets shot because the hearers don't like the message.

There are several levels of courage. There is animal

courage, human courage, and moral courage. A mother will rush into a burning building to rescue her child. A bomb disposal expert will need a very steady hand as he moves to disconnect the wires. And, lastly, a prophet will speak his/her truth, without fear or favour, just because of the moral courage that they have about their convictions. On a human level, life is so much easier and less complicated when we conform and avoid rocking the boat. Jesus didn't have to speak to the Samaritan woman, or touch the leper. He didn't have to heal the man on the Sabbath, or to sit down at table with sinners. And yet, as I write this, I know that this is not true! Yes, indeed, he had to, because of everything he was, and everything for which he stood. The very reason for his presence among us is seen at its sharpest focus, when we see exactly how and why he rebelled against the status quo.

If he allowed himself be hide-bound by the laws and customs of the time, he, too, would be in bondage. 'The Sabbath was made for the good of people, not people for the Sabbath', were his words. For the scribes and Pharisees, the law was paramount, and the only reason for their existence was to serve, fulfil, and obey the law. The teaching and behaviour of Jesus was totally at variance with everything they held dear. Jesus did not go around whispering his message in quiet corners. At his trial, he told them, 'What I teach is widely known, because I have preached regularly in the synagogues and the Temple. I have been heard by people everywhere, and I teach nothing in private that I have not said in public. Why are you asking me this question? Ask those who heard me. They know what I said.' This is courage and honesty of a very high order, and it became more and more evident that he would have to pay for this with his life. Part of being a rebel is a willingness to lay down one's life for the cause. Jesus declared this to be the highest form of love.

It would make a very interesting study if one were to paint in the background of the religion. expectations, and customs of Jesus' day, and then to overlay that with his actions and his teaching. Jesus was not being rebellious just for the sake of being so. As a matter of fact, he declared that 'I have not come to destroy the Law, but to fulfil it'. At first sight, that seems strange, and somewhat contradictory.

Law, in itself, should be there for the general good. If I have to slow down to thirty miles per hour while passing through a town, this is because it is in the best interests of all that I should do so. When I speak of law here, of course, I speak of a law that is just, and not there to oppress. A just law is there to protect and, even if I chaff or complain about its restrictions, I should be willing to accept the possibility that there are others involved in the situation besides myself. Observing just laws is a way of serving the common good. When I was growing up in the church, we had many laws that are no longer operative. They were there for a purpose and, when circumstances permitted, the laws could be altered, or removed entirely. Before we had concelebrated Masses, many of our larger churches might have many Masses going on at the same time, on side altars. Some people attached the greatest importance to the reception of Holy Communion, and, therefore, went from altar to altar, with the intention of receiving Communion as often as possible. This meant, for some of them, that they had not been present at one complete Mass! A rule was brought in, restricting Communion to once a day, and that put an end to their gallop!

This rule can now be rescinded because the circumstances are no longer the same. At the first Mass, it was 'after they had eaten' that Jesus instituted eucharist, celebrated the first Mass, and offered himself to them as food and drink. It wasn't long after that that Paul calls on the people to have their eating and drinking done before they leave home to come to celebrate eucharist, because some of them were known to have too much drink taken before eucharist began. To correct this abuse, the law of fasting before Communion was introduced; and this law can also be rescinded, when the need no longer exists. (In more recent times, we have witnessed the virtual disappearance of midnight Mass at Christmas and Easter, because the time coincided with the closing of the local pubs, when there often resulted a conflict of spirits!)

Because Jesus had come to fulfil the law, a great deal of the law was no longer necessary. The Ten Commandments were to be replaced by the Two Commandments of Love – for God, and for neighbour. If the religious leaders saw the law as a path to God then, in Jesus, God had come among them in person, and he himself would be the only path back to the garden. In doing this, Jesus had stood everything on its head, because it was God who made the journey towards us, rather than us struggling to get to him.

The observance of a just law should bring a benefit to the observers. The law should never be an end in itself; rather should it be the means to an end. Throughout all of the Old Testament, God should have been the end, purpose, and sole reason for the law. Jesus had now arrived, so things had come full circle. I think, in fairness to the Pharisees, it is not very realistic to expect them to understand or accept that! Their whole purpose for being was on the line, and we shouldn't be surprised that they would fight with great ferocity to protect their vital interests.

To be a Christian is to be a rebel, in the best sense of that word. Jesus came as a sign, 'as a sign of contradiction'. He spoke to the world of other values, of other ways of being and of doing. The whole purpose of Christian living is its witness value. 'You shall be my witnesses to the ends of the earth', he told his apostles. The greatest struggle for the Christian is to avoid being contaminated and polluted by the values and mores of the world. The life of the Christian doesn't make much sense to those with a worldy mind-set. Turning the other cheek, and forgiving seventy times seven, is utter foolishness to such people.

Salt, of itself, is not very appetising. It is only when mixed with something else that it can become a flavour, or a preservative. A lit candle is seen to best effect in darkness. Jesus said that Christians are to be the salt of the earth, and a light to the world. They must be seen, and they must effect the very atmosphere in which they live and breathe. They must light a candle, rather than curse the darkness. They must always witness to a higher value, to a more loving way of being and of acting. Unless the Spirit of God is active within the heart of the Christian, providing the enthusiasm of the prophet, the witness value of the living will wane, and end up as nothing different from that of the world. The Christian must be a rebel at heart, someone who 'hungers and thirsts after justice'. A Christian is on a mission, and, like Jesus, 'how can I be at peace until it be accomplished?'

14 The Outcast

'Show me your company, and I'll tell you what kind of person you are', is something that I often heard during my schooldays. I always accepted that as being true. Now, however, when I apply such a criterion to Jesus, it falls completely apart! To use human language in a literal sense, the process of Incarnation was one of absolute and total humility on the part of God. I say this with great reservation, however, because, in fact, I see it as one of extraordinary love.

Love will go to any lengths and, indeed, to any depths, to give expression to its existence. Love, by definition, is always active, is always engaged, is always giving. This is attitudinal, and not always in a tangible, evident way. Adam and Eve became outcasts when they were cast out of the garden. Their actions resulted in this, and it was of their own doing. They had been given free will, and they were free to leave or stay, to rebel or to obey. The consequent history of humanity after that was one of a nomadic people, without roots, wandering over the face of the earth. In our own society, unfortunately, there is a low level of acceptance for the nomad and the restless, unsettled traveller. In some way they are seen as outcasts, as not belonging, as being outside the pale. This is a two-edged sword. To resolve this, there must be movement on both sides of the spectrum. There must be an acceptance of the principle of 'live, and let live', allowing that each of us shares this earth with equal right. The travelling community must be allowed decide whether they want to settle, or preserve their customs and tradition, and the settled community must be prepared to respect the rights of such people to live and exist. Long long before I can be prepared to allow such people settle anywhere near where I live, I must honestly accept their basic right to exist in the first place! Intolerance is the inability to tolerate, and it comes from prejudice, which is a word for pre-judging. It is passing judgement, without actually being in possession of all the facts. Empathy is the ability to unscrew the top of another's head, look out from there, and see things as that person sees them. I am not pretending to be so idealistic as to suggest that we should all naturally be this way! With our own human nature, this is completely impossible for us.

There is an old Irish phrase that translates as 'God spoke first'. God did it through Jesus and, through the Spirit, he makes it possible for us to do it. Lucifer was cast out of heaven. God, in Jesus, willingly left heaven to come down here among us. 'He did not cling to equality with God, but became as we are.' 'He who was without sin, became sin for us.' Like Thompson's 'The Hound of Heaven', Jesus pursued us, as it were; he came into exile with us, so he could lead us back home.

It is impossible for the human mind to comprehend the full implications and ramifications of Incarnation. One of the core concepts of Christianity is that, for life to be gained, it must be given away. 'Unless the grain of wheat dies, it remains alone.' The grain of wheat must shrivel and die if there is to be a new stalk of wheat above the ground. If I look at things from the perspective of the worm, I will only see dead and shrivelled seeds and bulbs, and have no idea of what that dying has produced.

We are all familiar with the idea of upstairs/downstairs, and of the social levels represented by both. In a society like India, the caste-system is more evident. There is a line over which some people can never hope to cross. Being born 'on the wrong side of the tracks' is one way we have of expressing this. From the moment of his birth in a stable, Jesus was outside the echelons of power, influence, and respectability.

While still a child, he became a refugee in Egypt. The idea of being a homeless refugee is something that is all too familiar in today's world. He would later declare that 'the foxes have holes, the birds have nests, but the Son of Man has nowhere to lay his head'. Like anyone in a lower caste, Jesus didn't own anything. Riches and wealth are often confused. Riches has little to do with money. I could possess much wealth, and be a really poor person. What I am, and what I possess are two totally different entities. In the eyes of his neighbours, Jesus was the son of a carpenter. When the power of God began to manifest itself through him, many of his neighbours were puzzled and, indeed, downright angry. How dare he pretend to be anything other than who they saw him to be! We are all familiar with the exclamation, 'Just who does she thinks she is?'

The actual conditions in which Jesus lived are not easily understood, with human comprehension. Of course, he was God; always was, and ever will be. What happened, actually, was that he put his divinity totally to one side, and took on our humanity, with all the consequences that flow from that. It would be wrong to think of Jesus carrying his divinity around, under cover, until needed! I suggest that he put aside every personal claim to Godhead, and to all the strengths and powers that go with that. It was not until the Holy Spirit came upon him in the Jordan river that he had access to a Higher Power. This was very important, because it was thus that he ordained that we also should come into the fulness of divinity, when our baptism in the Holy Spirit would take place. 'Greater things than this shall you do ...'

We are all children of Adam and, because of original sin, we are all outcasts. We have nothing of ourselves that can change that condition in any way. Jesus went to great lengths to show his attitude towards the outcast and the marginalised. He was a friend to the natural 'enemy', whether that be a Samaritan or a Roman officer, and he touched the untouchables. Even if he had been born within the caste of respectability, he would have totally alienated himself by such actions. It was obvious that he acted in this way with full awareness of what he was doing, and the consequences of such actions. On several occasions, the leaders attempted to stone him to death, something that was the penalty reserved for such undesirables. Death by crucifixion was the ultimate shameful penalty for the most notorious outcasts. Calvary was the clearest and most definitive declaration of how the religious leaders saw Jesus, and thought of him. When the leaders and soldiers came to arrest him, Jesus said, 'Am I some dangerous criminal that you have come armed with swords and clubs to arrest me?' Yes, indeed, in their eyes, he was someone who presented a real danger to them. He didn't belong. He refused to play the game their way, to conform, to know and keep his place; therefore, they had to 'put him in his place.'

When Jesus was nailed to the cross, the whole truth of his being an outcast was most evident, and most graphically displayed. Crucifixion was reserved for slaves and foreigners. It was considered not only the most painful form of death, but an annihilation of the person. The victim's name could never again be spoken without shame. At that time it seemed to Jesus that even the Father had deserted him. The apostles had run away, not wanting to share in his shame and failure. He had been mocked, jeered at, and stripped in public. All human help had evaporated, apart from a few very loyal, but helpless friends. And then, all sense of connection was severed, and he felt totally alone. At that moment, he experienced himself as irreprievably outcast from both earth and heaven. He had a sense of being hanging there between earth and heaven, as if disowned by both. 'Freedom's just another word for nothing left to lose' is a nice concept, while being a very frightening reality.

There is no form of human agony or pain that Jesus did not experience to the limits. He was paying the price for the sins of the world, and, therefore, the extent and the depth of the struggle would be such as to be inclusive of all the ills and all the pains of humanity. Even in death he was not free from the taunts and the jeers. This came even from someone who was sentenced to die with him. The Old Testament prophesies are replete with the cries of the wounded one, the unwanted one, the outcast among the people. It was as if he had to become the greatest outcast of all times so as to reach those most alienated, and most marginalised. This was love being poured out gratuitously, and in abundance, and the world has never, and will never, witness such love again.

Jesus warned his disciples, 'They have hated me, so they will hate you. Blessed are you when people persecute you, and speak ill of you, because of me.' The whole scenario and the message is so foreign to the expectations of the world that, in the words of Paul, 'to the Jews it is foolishness, and to the Greeks a scandal'. In dressing him up in robes of mockery, and crowning him with a crown of thorns, the soldiers were meting out the treatment they saw that he deserved. He was a fool by any standards, and deserved to be treated as one.

Paul speaks of 'becoming a fool for Christ's sake'. We are all familiar with the situation where people who take the gospel seriously are generally suspect, at least in the eyes of many. I'm not speaking of religious eccentrics here. The world would prefer much greater caution, prudence, and earthly common-sense. It is important to always be in control, and always be seen to be in control. To become the voice of the poor, the voice of the voiceless, is to risk persecution, and alienation. Right down to this day we know of people who have forfeited their lives, because they dared to stand up against the so-called wisdom of the world. 'In the eyes of the world, they seemed to have died, but for those who believe, they have entered into eternal glory.' The kingdom of Jesus is not of this world, and the values of that kingdom could never conform to the expectations of this world.

If Jesus were to save the world, he could never become part of it. That he should be an outcast, to be seen as an outcast, and to be treated as such, all of this was part of God's plan for the redemption of the world. He joined us in our deepest darkness, and led us out into the light, into the freedom of the children of God. This is the message of the church to the homeless, the marginalised, the disenfranchised: 'You are important, and that is why we want to help you. You may be seen as outcasts in the eyes of the world, but, because of Jesus, you are ranked among the most precious of God's children.'

15 The Martyr

A martyr is someone who undergoes death for any great cause, and this cause usually has to do with religious convictions, loyalty to the teachings of one's church, or to correct some glaring injustice. This is very far removed from the person who dies in the pursuit of some personal gain, such as trying to get wealthy by robbing a bank. There has always been a sacredness attached to the blood of the martyr, because blood is so central to life that, to pour this out for another is an act of courage, love, and loyalty of the highest degree.

Sacrifice has always been associated with an offering made to God. This extends to all beliefs, whatever the god. Because we speak of God as being love in essence, the sacrifice is in response to his love, or to bring ourselves under the graciousness of that love, if it is felt that we have alienated ourselves from it. Even the blood of a lamb that was sacrified to God was sufficient to protect the houses of the Israelites from the angel of death and destruction. When they sacrificed a lamb or a bull to their God, these people were sometimes sprinkled with the blood as a token of their belonging, and as a sign of their adherence to the covenant which God had made with them.

A sacrifice involves the slaughter or destruction of something, which is offered to God as a token of thanksgiving, repentance, or reparation. This was one of the core ways the Hebrews had of worshipping God. This sacrifice ranged from a lamb to a bull or bullock. The animal was killed, the blood was poured out in a ritual, and the carcass was then totally burned, as the smoke ascended like prayer before their God.

A genuine sacrifice meant the total offering of all that the animal represented. For example, God accused the people of 'committing rapine in the holocaust', which meant that, while the flesh was burning, some of them were tempted, and they sliced off portions of the animal to eat. This desecrated the whole concept of a 'whole-burned-offering', something that was considered sacred and sacrosanct. Such offerings played a large part in their prayer of repentance and surrender to God. The animal being sacrified was in lieu of themselves and, like any ritual, the external procedures were but an attempt to illustrate what should be going on in the heart. I'm sure someone has counted the number of times the word *sacrifice* is used in the Old Testament alone. I would venture to say that it is more frequent than the word God, or Yahweh, as the Hebrews called God.

As I said, the idea of blood being poured out was at the core of sacrifice. This was an emptying, a total giving, complete surrender, and the word normally used was 'libation'. When we come to consider the whole question of the death of Jesus, it is very important that we situate it within this wider context of sacrifice and libation. Right at the beginning of Jesus' public ministry, John the Baptist called him the Lamb of God. Not only would his blood be poured out for the forgiveness of sin, but for the sin of the world. We pray, 'Lamb of God, who takes away the sins of the world, have mercy on us.' His was a sacrifice to end all sacrifices. It could be renewed, of course, it could be offered again and again, and that is what we call eucharist or Mass. This does not mean that Jesus dies again every time I offer Mass. 'Jesus Christ, having died once for sin, now reigns in glory at the right hand of the Father.' Every time a Mass is offered, the prayer, the 'yes' of Jesus that was offered on Calvary, is offered yet again, except that, this time, I now can offer my 'yes' to Jesus with his 'yes' to the Father. In that way, the Mass becomes a 'perpetual sacrifice' that can be renewed and offered 'from east to west' for all time. 'By his blood we are saved … by his

blood we are forgiven … by his blood we are washed clean.'
This is the recurring theme in the New Testament letters, especially from Paul. The head-long struggle Jesus had with the
religious leaders of his day can raise its nasty head here
again. Because of the blood of Jesus, salvation is a gratuitous
free gift. Paul sums it up in the following words from
Romans 3:

> But now God has shown us a different way of being right
> in his sight … We are made right in God's sight when we
> trust in Jesus Christ to take away our sins. And we can all
> be saved in the same way, no matter who we are, or what
> we have been like. For all have sinned, all fall short of
> God's glorious standard. Yet now God in his gracious
> kindness declares us not guilty. He has done this through
> Jesus Christ, who has freed us by taking away our sins.
> For God sent Jesus to take the punishment for our sins,
> and to satisfy God's anger against us. We are made right
> with God when we believe that Jesus shed his blood, sacri-
> ficing his life for us.

Another translation speaks of 'Christ's blood and our faith'
as being the formula for salvation. There is nothing automatic
at all in this. The first part is what Jesus has done, and the second part, also important, is whether we believe and accept
that or not.

I said earlier that a martyr is someone who dies for a good
cause. Jesus became a martyr for us, and the good cause is
our salvation. Prophets often tended to end up as martyrs,
because of the antagonism their words provoke. All of Jesus'
life led him inexorably to martyrdom. It was not a question of
giving till it hurt, but of giving till it's gone. It was total love,
it was total giving. The very ground on which we walk has
been blessed by the blood of the martyrs that soaked into it.
Out of the death of martyrs came whole new life, something
that has been witnessed to again and again throughout history. Because of this total outpouring of Jesus, many special
souls, such as Thérèse of Liseux, had a very strong desire for

martyrdom. They felt that nothing less would satisfy their burning desire to give themselves to someone who had given himself so totally to them. All of this is sheer stupidity and waste, in the eyes of the world. And yet, we must ask, is it?

The hero-worshipping of martyrs has not always been based on religious grounds alone. Every nation has had its martyrs, even if history shows their zeal to be subversive or misguided. While Jesus extols the merits of fasting, there have been those who have used hunger-strikes as a weapon of resistance and defiance. In the Christian tradition, the martyrs were always considered as saints, even before they are officially canonised. Indeed, in the catechism of my school-days, martyrdom was deemed as being fully effective in the forgiveness of all sins, and of all debts outstanding to God. I'm not sure that this would be readily acceptable today, because the very willingness to lay down one's life for a just cause must surely betoken an already special relationship with God.

In considering the death of Jesus, it is important for us to remember that this was God who chose to die for us, so that he could lead us into a whole new possibility of living. This was the Red Sea once again except, this time, it is made red by the blood of God incarnate. This is the Way into life, and nobody can come to God except through this sacrifice of Jesus. His blood washes sin away, it pays the price for redeeming the slave, it overcomes all the bondages represented by inhabiting the human body. When the human body of Jesus was emptied of everything, both blood and water, it was then restored to the fulness of divinity, and was placed beyond the reach of all earthly destruction and decay.

On a human level, the death of Jesus was a disaster while, with the eyes and with logic of God, it was eternally triumphant. His death was a sin-offering in the complete and total meaning of that word. 'By his wounds we are healed', Paul tells us. The death of Jesus is 'the one and eternal sacrifice offered for sin'. As the blood of the lamb protected the homes of the Hebrews, so the blood of Jesus opened the gates of heaven for God's people. It is significant that, just as he died, the graves were opened, the dead arose and appeared to many, and the veil of the Temple was rent in two. For the first time ever, it is possible for us to enter into the Holy of Holies.

When the leaders met to discuss what to do about Jesus, to silence him, the High priest spoke some prophetic words, 'Is it not right that one man should die for the people, rather than the whole nation be destroyed?' 'This prophecy that Jesus should die for the entire nation came from Caiaphus in his position as high priest. He didn't think of it himself; he was inspired to say it. It was a prediction that Jesus' death would not be for Israel only, but for the gathering together of all the children of God scattered all around the world.' While John tells us that the words of Caiaphus were prophetic, he probably underestimated the powerful prophetic nature of his own words, just quoted.

To become a follower of Jesus is to set out on the path of dying, and of rising to new life. Dying for Christians is what happens during their life-time. Love for others means dying to self. Death is like a pile of sand at the end of life, that the Christian can take and sprinkle, a few grains at a time, along the journey of life. If I wait till the end of my life to die, it could well be too late. This daily dying to self, whether it be my opinions, my possessions, or my comforts, is what Jesus calls his cross. This is a word that is not too well understood. Losing a job, suffering a stroke, or having a child born with a mental or physical handicap is often referred to as 'a great cross'. While not wishing to be insensitive, I have to say that this is not true. Such things happen to pagans as well, whereas the cross is uniquely Christian. Such things can be seen as a blessing, or they can be seen as a curse. The cross, on the other hand, is always redemptive, is always a blessing, is always life-giving. Jesus said that, to be a disciple of his, we have to take up our cross every day and follow him. The cross consists of every act and of every word that results directly from my decision to follow Jesus, and to obey him. If I am a Christian, I have to forgive you, to help you, and to love you. Generally speaking, it is not a heavy cross, being made up of splinters, as it were, rather than any great oppressing burden. 'My yoke is easy, and my burden is light'.

Jesus' commitment to martyrdom was sealed when he entered the Jordan waters, with the sins of the world on his shoulders. The Christian begins the journey with a ceremony involving water. That waters returns, one drop at a time, every time the Christian offers the sacrifice of Jesus in eucharist. The chalice represents the death of Jesus. 'Father, if it is possible, let this chalice pass from me ...' Before offering the chalice of Jesus' death to the Father, the priest puts in a drop of water to represent the daily-dyings that are part and parcel of Christian living.

In the spirituality of the Fathers of the Church, martyrdom covered more than actually dying. There was martyrdom of desire, such as was the longing of Thérèse of Liseux, and there was what was called the 'white maryrdom of the celibate virginal life', when everything that was most vital and central to one's existence as a person was sacrificed for the service of God, and the building up of his kingdom. 'Leave everything, and follow me' is the stark invitation of Jesus. In doing so, I am following a martyred leader, and my life as a Christian must always include and contain a certain element of martyrdom in it. Most of us will never have to make the supreme sacrifice for the gospel but, because we are marked with the blood of the Lamb, we take on the vocation of dying so that we can be born into eternal life.

16 The Victor

The ultimate sin for the Christian is to lose hope. Because of what Jesus has done, we can live with the certainty that evil can never triumph, even if seen to be successful for a time. The Stalins and the Hitlers of this world will come and go, and life will continue without them. In human terms, Calvary was total and dismal failure but, because of the resurrection that followed, a whole new way of looking at things begins to emerge. God, in a way, is an upside-down God! Thomas Aquinas said that when you speak of God, you can be sure of just one thing: you are wrong! No matter how good, how powerful, or how loving you think he is, he is much much more than that. He is the Creator, and, therefore, he can recreate that which is destroyed or damaged. Heaven is a state of permanent praise, of exultation, and of triumphant joy. The victory of Jesus will reverberate for all eternity. Everything will be set right, from Lucifer, to Adam and Eve, to our day. The prince of this world will be bound for all eternity, and his kingdom will have come to an end. The kingdom of this world, with its wrong priorities and false gods, will have ended and there will remain the kingdom of God, and that alone.

In an earlier chapter I referred to a movie I saw some years ago called *Love Story*. It was a beautiful and touching story, but it was different from most movies in that it began with the end of the story, where the heroine was seen to die. The movie then went back to tell the story from the beginning. As I watch the story unfolding, I already know the outcome, and I follow the story with that in mind. This is a dimension of

Christian living, because of what Jesus has done. His journey ended in victory and triumph, and so will ours, if we choose to follow me. 'If you follow me, you will not walk in darkness, but will have the light of life.' The Christian can live with the sounds of Alleluias in her ears. Such a one can raise her eyes to the stars, and see beyond the dust and dirt of the road. 'We have not here a lasting city, but we look for one that is to come.' 'This world is not my home; I'm just a-passing through' are the words of a country and western song.

What God created was good, and God himself saw that, and said that. If nothing had happened to adversely affect that, we would still be in the garden. Sin, sickness, and death are not of God's creation. These are pollutants and evils that entered with original sin. When the labourers asked the farmer about the weeds that appeared among the good wheat he had sown, he said that 'an enemy has done this'. When they offered to pull up the weeds, he told them not to. He would attend to that himself because, in pulling up the weeds, they ran the risk of destroying the wheat as well. It was to overcome and remove the evils of sin, sickness, and death that Jesus came. In other chapters in this book I have written about how he set out to do this, and how he achieved this. Beyond mentioning it, I do not intend restating all of that again. What I wish to do now is examine the practical ramifications for us, resulting from the victory won for us by Jesus.

The simplest way to summarise the victory of Jesus is to say that he made it possible for us to return to the garden. I often think that, back in the garden, God would not have needed preachers and teachers to proclaim his message, because, by the nature of their living, everyone would be fully aware of all that, and fully conscious of how all of that was evident to them. Salvation is not something I get when I die; rather is it the grace to start again any day I so wish. Salvation for us is that we can return to the garden and begin all over again. We can walk with God in the cool of the evenings, and be fully conscious of his presence and his care at all times. I am not ignoring the realities of daily living, with all the struggles that go with that. What I am saying is that, because of what Jesus has done, none of that can ever be the same again. 'You are not alone, my friend, anymore.' 'I am with you always. I will never abandon you, or leave you in the storm. My Spirit will lead you, and will remain with you always.' We can consider and celebrate as much as we like all that Jesus has done for us, but it all becomes totally empty and lifeless unless we actually live and experience the results of what he has done.

I said in a previous chapter that God was an upside-down God. It is as if his roots were in heaven, that he grows downwards, more and more towards us, and that the fruits are all within our reach. In that sense, he is a totally down-to-earth God. A fourteenth-century writer tells us that 'The seeker must climb the tree of faith, which grows downwards from above, since its roots are in the Godhead.' We are the ones who can reap the harvest of all Jesus has sown and, indeed, we ourselves are the fruits of that harvest. 'You are my glory', he says, as he speaks of presenting us to the Father as the ultimate fruits of victory. Jesus has regained for the Father 'the lost sheep of the House of Israel'. The one fold, and the one shepherd is his ultimate goal, even if many are called, but not all choose to heed that call. He wept as he overlooked the city of Jerusalem. 'Salvation was within your grasp, but you would not accept it.' At Mass we say 'By your cross and resurrection you have set us free; you are the Saviour of the world.' There is a very serious onus on us to fully grasp and avail of that freedom. It is not unrealistic to suggest that the greatest torment of hell is to clearly see that salvation was within our grasp, and we did not accept it.

It is very significant that Jesus spent so much time with his disciples after his resurrection. This was his final victory, his victory over the final enemy, and it was absolutely essential that they be convinced beyond all doubt of the reality of that victory. Their main task was to witness to the fact of his resurrection. Crucifixion was for slaves and foreigners, and those who suffered such a death were never to be mentioned by name again. Imagine the horror of the Jewish leaders when they heard the apostles going around speaking about Jesus, and claiming that he had risen from the dead! They were strictly forbidden 'to speak in that Name again'. Peter and John replied to such an order with the words, 'We cannot stop talking about the wonderful things we have seen and heard.' In a way, I suppose, the religious leaders began to feel like people on a beach, trying to hold back the tide with a spoon! This Jesus just wouldn't go away!

There was a way in which this man, his teachings, his memory, and now his presence, just could not be halted. Without understanding and accepting the reality of resurrection, one can readily empathise with their confusion. This mystery was so unearthly, so unreal in human terms, so impossible to human thinking, that even the apostles were forbidden by Jesus to speak publicly about it until after the Spirit came. 'Stay in Jerusalem until the Spirit comes, and fills you with power from on high. Then you will become my witnesses to the ends of the earth.' It was something that God did, and only God could understand. It was something that was so intrinsically of God, that only God himself could proclaim it. This he would do through his Spirit working within those who would be anointed. At the beginning of his earthly ministry, after his baptism in the Jordan, Jesus said that 'the Spirit of God has been given to me. I have been anointed, and sent to bring good news to the poor, to bring light to those in darkness.'

Jesus proclaimed his victory over Satan, the father of lies, and he sent his Spirit of truth to lead us into all truth, and 'the truth will set you free'. His resurrection was victory over death, but it also represented a victory over the evil forces that brought about that death. He had come to establish and to proclaim the kingdom of God, and he announced that his kingdom would remain when all other kingdoms had fallen, and ceased to be.

He laid great emphasis on the totality of his victory. 'All authority is given me in heaven and on earth.' He came to bring love, to generate faith, and to give hope. 'In his victory is our hope.' Peter tells the early Christians, 'Always have an explanation ready to give to those who ask you the reason for the hope that you have.' Implied in this is the expectation that to be a Christian is to be someone with an eternal hope.

For each of us, of course, the times in which we happen to inhabit the earth can seem to be the 'best of times, and the worst of times', in the words of Dickens. There is a certain air of despondency in the world today, on many issues. Nowhere is this more evident than in church circles. This is one of those quirks of contradiction that can bedevil the lives of the best of us. Of ourselves, we see with the eyes of the body, and are basically very blind to the way things really are. We tend to count, while God tends to weigh; we are interested in length, while God is more interested in depth. We count our prayers, and we tend to judge our lives by the length of years lived. Most of us grew up in a church which was safe, secure, unquestioned, and unchallenged. We knew no other way of being, and of belonging. This is how it is, and this is how it will and must remain. Today, however, into our present situation must come all the central tenets of the gospel about dying before resurrection is possible, about being pruned back for further growth, about being seen and treated as something insignificant and transient in the eyes of the world. Much and many of our fears can have pride at their hearts. We may no longer be a force to be reckoned with, a church commanding and demanding respect and allegiance, and something that is essentially revelant in the lives of common people.

Never before, in my own lifetime at least, have I had to sharpen my vision of hope, and to examine the reality of that hope. Jesus said that his church would be founded on a rock, but he also told us to build our faith on a rock, rather than on sand; otherwise, when the storms come, the whole edifice can come tumbling down around us, 'and what a fall that will be'. The church is the Body of Christ. The Body of Christ is beyond the grasp of death. The problem with the Body of Christ, however, is that it just keeps changing all the time! The apostles, disciples, and Mary Magdalene knew Jesus by sight very well and, yet, from the moment of resurrection, they seemed to be totally confused as to what he looked like! The apostles thought he was a ghost, Mary Magdalene thought he was a gardener, and the disciples on the road to Emmaus thought he was a tourist.

The problem with the church in the last few hundred years is that it tried to remain the same, to become predictable, to become so 'Catholic' as to have a universal language, and to return in some way to the level of the scribes and Pharisees in its emphasis on law. Vatican II brought all of that to an end in a most prophetic way, and history will show just how providential and how prophetic John XXIII really was.

To live with hope is to live with change, with constant change. 'My God is new with every new day', Cardinal Suenens wrote. Freud said that the test of a person's maturity is his ability to survive in a state of ambiquity. We instinctively like certainties that insulate us against our insecurities. Jesus said that 'the sin of this world is unbelief in me'. While genuine concern, consideration, and effort should be brought to bear in establishing and building up the Body of Christ in the world, all that smacks of despair or doomsday prophecy is resultant from that lack of faith. 'The gates of hell will not prevail against it' is Jesus' promise to his church. 'Heaven and earth will pass away before my word will pass away', he promises us. Jesus was willing to let go of everything, his divinity, and his very life. It is difficult, of course, to let go but I believe that the Christian of today must be willing to let go of many of the sacred cows of yesterday. 'Behold, I make all things new', says the Lord. I believe it would be a wonderful freedom, a very real level of wholeness, and of holiness, and a truly humble submission to God, to be able to pray, 'Lord, take what you want, even the church that I have known, if such be your will. Not my will but yours be done. Just give me, please, the freedom to be nothing so that, in you, and in you alone, will I have everything. Please help me accept that the church is your responsibility; you know what you're doing, you know what is best. Just lead me, through your Spirit, in whatever way you wish me to serve your people in the world of today.'

The letter to the Hebrews speaks of 'the sure and certain hope' that every Christian should have. Jesus has overcome the enemy. 'Nothing shall harm you. Your names are registered as citizens of heaven', he tells us. When we speak of Jesus, we often use the past tense. For example, 'Dying you destroyed our death; rising you restored our life. By your cross and resurrection you have set us free ...' The task is completed, the victory is won. All that is needed is that the victory be proclaimed. My role is not to save souls, but to tell people that they are saved. Because the core value of Christianity is its witness value, it becomes really important that Christians begin to *look* saved! Christianity is about attracting rather than promoting. If I were to write down all the possible evils, and all the major problems that could befall a human being, I would have a veritable back-breaking burden of impossibilities, and of elements of destruction. As a Christian, however, I should begin with what Jesus has done, with what he has acccomplished, and view everything else against that background. 'My grace is sufficient for you. I will never lead you where my grace and my Spirit will not be there to see you through'.

To live as a Christian is to live with victory, and to give witness to the reality of that victory. At the time of writing I have just returned from Lourdes, after the annual handicapped children's pilgrimage. Everything I saw there was filled with hope, because it was wrapped in love. There were no children there who were not deemed precious, even though, from a human point of view in the case of some, there was little evident purpose in their living. Hope is living with the certainty that, no matter how things may seem to be now, 'all will be well, and all manner of things will be well'. Like the movie *Love Story*, we should consider the end purpose and destiny of our lives, and then return to the living of that life. Jesus came that we should have life, and have it in abundance. That is the essence of his victory.

17 The Judge

It doesn't require any great theological exploration to accept the simple fact that, if Jesus came to save us, if he is the door to the sheepfold, if he is the only Way to the Father, that he should require something from us by way of accepting, believing, and acting on his instructions. 'If you love me, you will obey me.' Judging, such as some form of judgement at death, or a general judgement at the end of time, must not be confused with our understanding of judging in the secular and legal sense. God doesn't send me anywhere when I die; rather does he eternalise the direction in which I now travel. The essence of judgement is in my own hands. Jesus says that he will not have to judge us, in that the words he has spoken will judge us. If he had not come and spoken we would have an excuse for our sins. Many theologians argue that, even after the moment of death, when I am free of the body and able to see myself relative to God, to others, and to the reality of my situation, that I will be given one last chance to say 'yes' or 'no'. This would answer the many legitimate questions about two thirds of the human race who know nothing about Jesus, or about his message; and about someone whose death is instantaneous, as a result of violence, for example, as against those who have every spiritual and medical care for a long time before death.

Whatever God's judgement will be, we can be sure and certain that it will be absolutely and totally just and, if it were to lean in any direction, it will certainly lean towards the side of the sinner. If we say that God possesses all qualities in an infinite way, then we must accept that he is infinitely just. A general overview of the larger canvas could well envisage the possibility of something like this: In creation, God opened up an era of total and unconditional love. We rejected this, so, in Jesus, he opened up an era of total mercy and forgiveness. Is it possible that this will be followed by a time of total justice, when each of us will reap the harvest of whatever we have sown? Even in this, I must hold to the belief that God's love and mercy will not have come to an end. Our hope has to be eternal, because it is invested in an eternal God.

There is some innate way in which the law of God is imprinted on our hearts. The most primitive tribe believed in a god, even if they adored the sun. They believed in an afterlife, even if they called it the spirit world, Valhalla, or crossing the Jordan. When I was a child I had a dog that looked guilty whenever he did something wrong! When a person dies, one of the first things the attendant staff do is to close the eyes and the mouth. It is as if the eyes of the soul can see clearly now, and the voice of the heart can express the deepest words.

I personally have no problem whatsoever with a God who would offer a final choice to the one who can now see things as they really are. I believe, however, that I just cannot presume on saying that final 'yes', if it has not been preceded by the many 'yeses' of daily living, loving, and service. I know that it can raise questions about the total and absolute authority of God, but I believe that if Satan were offered such a final choice, he would refuse; because to repent would mean admitting that he was wrong in the first place, and I don't believe his pride could permit of such a thing.

Matthew's gospel, chapter 25, provides us with a fairly detailed discourse from Jesus on what is called the Final Judgement. For the religious person, it must appear to be scandalously materialistic! There are no questions there about church-going, religious experiences, or exercises of devotion. The questions have to do with food, drink, clothes, compassion, and hospitality in general. There is quite a huge canvas background to this scenario. The sheep are those who follow the shepherd, and the goats are the ones who are driven, without any sense of loyalty. Judgement is described as separating the sheep from the goats. 'You are either for me, or against me. Let your yes be yes, and your no be no', Jesus had said at an earlier time. Goodness is seen as attitudinal, as a way of living, because those whom he commends are surprised; they lived and behaved that way because that is the kind of people they had become. 'At the end of the day', says Jesus, 'you are but unprofitable servants, doing that which is your duty to do'. In this judgement Jesus is not rewarding the just, as if they have earned or merited something. Rather is he looking within their souls and proclaiming what he sees and knows to be there. 'Nathaniel, when you were under the fig tree I saw you' was a comment that surprised more than just Nathaniel at the very beginning of Jesus' ministry.

Judgement is more about what Jesus means when he declares that all will be made public, all will be revealed. There is nothing hidden from the eyes of God and, with our new-found vision, we will all be capable of seeing things as they really are. Jesus said that he did not come to condemn the world, but to save it. I certainly don't think of this judgement as being a process of condemnation. I can accept that, even at this final moment, as with Satan, some people will still refuse the offer of God. God doesn't give me anything; rather he offers me everything, and I must always have the freedom to accept or reject. Even at that last moment, he would never deprive me of my free will.

Of one thing we can be sure. When we return to the garden, the Father will be waiting with open arms to welcome all of his prodigal children. Jesus uses many parables to teach us about this final round-up of God's people. He compares it to a net that is cast into the sea. When the net is brought ashore, the fish are selected, and what is not fish is discarded. Is it possible that God will scoop up what is good in us, and dispose of the rest? Leonard Cheshire suggests the possibility of a meeting at the moment of death between the person I then will be, and the person God created me to be. Because my definition of love states that love is accepting another as that person is, I can trust God's love to accept me as I then will be. Jesus speaks of a wedding feast, where one person showed up inappropriately dressed, and was quickly dismissed from the gathering. Because of his love for the poor, it is unthinkable that there is any implication here that the person was too poor to be dressed properly. Obviously, he knew how he should be dressed, and he also had whatever it took to conform to the norm. There is the implication of some sort of stubborn perversity that resulted in him bringing judgement upon his own head.

There is a subject called Eschatology, which has to do with teaching about death, judgement, hell, and heaven. One element of this is the following premise: all of this is here now, a present reality, but not entirely yet. In other words, the road to heaven is heaven, and the road to hell is hell, and I can open my heart and soul to God's judgement each and every day. It is more than just coming events throwing their shadow. The Jesus with whom I will come face to face at death is the very same Jesus I can follow each day, and to whom I can now belong. Jesus told the apostles that those who leave all things to follow him will themselves join with him in judging 'the twelve tribes of Israel'.

If we are to absorbed into Jesus, to become one with him, there must surely be a possibility that we may be involved in the judging, if only of ourselves. In our present journey, Jesus asks us not to judge, so that we may not be judged. He speaks of those who will pass to the fullness of life without being judged. He prays to the Father to keep them safe, and he promises them that he will come to bring them, so that where he is, they also will be. I believe the final judgement will have more to do with the proclamation of the eternal victory of Jesus, rather than the condemnation of sinners.

I said in an earlier paragraph, of course, that we will still have our free will, that we will still be free to make choices. We can only trust his Spirit to effect such a transformation in us, that, like Mary, it would not be in our nature to rebel against God. Mary was conceived without sin. I believe, however, that, even if she were not, her humility alone would have prevented her from ever being so arrogant as to challenge the Almighty God. Sin is pride that leads to disobedience. We can trust Jesus to have removed this weed from among the good wheat of our souls and, in the words of an old Irish song 'we will all be gathered in the great harvest of God'.

I already quoted another old Irish saying, meaning that 'God spoke first'. In the judgement, the final word is with Jesus. He is the Alpha and the Omega, the beginning and the end. 'It is not the will of your heavenly Father that any of you should be lost.' Isaiah speaks of the Holy Highway that is opened up in the desert. The redeemed will walk along it, singing songs of grateful praise and of everlasting joy, as they return to Jerusalem.' The Book of Revelations speaks of heaven as the New Jerusalem. Throughout the Bible, Jerusalem is seen as the heartland of home. Jesus leads us to that home. This is pure and total gift. It is never something that can be earned or merited. I have only one claim and that is the life, the message, and the promises of Jesus Christ. In a literal sense, I stake my salvation on those promises.

In the Acts of the Apostles, there are several lengthy discources about Jesus, all of which is loudly proclaimed as good news. There are normally four parts in the message thus proclaimed: The Messiah has come; you killed him; he rose from the dead; and he will return in glory at the end of time. It is evident that this final and fourth part of the message is also seen and proclaimed as good news. The return of the Jesus they had lived with, and known, was indeed very good news. It was something they longed and prayed for and, indeed, it is abundantly evident that they hoped and expected that this would happen in their own lifetime. The very last word in the Bible is 'Maranatha , come Lord Jesus'.

I can trust the Lord, in the words of Paul, 'to complete the good work he has begun in me'. The Jesus of whom I have written in this book is not someone I fear. 'Do not be afraid' is repeated many many times throughout the gospels. John, in his first letter, writes:

> God is love, and all who live in love, live in God, and God lives in them. And, as we live in God, our love grows more perfect. So we will not be afraid on the Day of Judgement, but we can face him with confidence, because we are like Christ here in this world. Such love has no fear, because perfect love drives out all fear. If we are afraid it is because of judgement, and this shows that his love has not been perfected in us.

I accept totally that all judgement belongs to Jesus, because, as he said, the Father had given him all authority in heaven and on earth. From what I know of Jesus, and because of my trust in his love, I will willingly present myself before him, knowing that, at the end of the day, it is all total gift. I certainly would much prefer to be judged by Jesus than by people! Because of the burdens of guilt and self-condemnation I have laid on myself along the road of life, I have no reason to even trust myself!

I will end this by making my own that final cry of the Bible, 'Maranatha, come Lord Jesus!'